tasting along the wine road

cookbook

a collection of recipes from "A Wine & Food Affair"

cookbook **volume 10**

Recipes from the Wineries and Lodgings
of the Alexander, Dry Creek
and Russian River Valleys. The
Russian River Wine Road is in
Northwest Sonoma County, California.

A custom cookbook published by the
Russian River Wine Road
P.O. Box 46, Healdsburg, CA 95448

www.wineroad.com

Content © Russian River Wine Road

Design © Pembroke Studios, www.pembrokestudios.com
Unless noted, photos © Lenny Siegel, www.siegelphotographic.com
Photo on Front Cover © Rick Tang
Photo on Back Cover © Richard Pembroke
Photo of Truett Hurst Winery © Rob Scheid
Photo of Honor Mansion © Steve Aja
Thank you to the following members for submitting their photo:
Case Ranch Inn · Chalk Hill · Chateau Felice · Creekside Inn · DeLoach · Hanna · Jenner Inn · Shelford House · Sonoma Orchid Inn

ISBN 978-1-60643-873-2

Printed in China

table of contents

table of contents

table of contents

foreword

executive chef Jesse Mallgren

Madrona Manor Wine Country Inn & Restaurant, Healdsburg, CA

I grew up in Sonoma County, and every spring my family would plant a large vegetable garden. The first tomato I remember eating was plucked straight from the vine and sprinkled with just a touch of salt. It tasted like summer in my mouth.

I would wander through the rows of corn, eating the raw ears before the natural sugars turned to starch. In the fall, I would dig small red potatoes out of the black earth and take them to the kitchen. We would boil the potatoes, toss them with sea salt and butter, and eat them with fresh Dungeness crab from Bodega Bay.

After picking the summer's bounty, my family would braid garlic to use over the winter. Tomatoes would be canned or turned into catsup, to be enjoyed until the next year, when the cycle of planting, nurturing and harvesting would begin again.

At Madrona Manor, I'm blessed with a bountiful garden as well. Our fava beans are served within hours of being picked, when they are so sweet that they taste almost like candy. Fresh herbs snipped from outside the back door of the kitchen marry well with glistening halibut pulled from local waters. Free-range eggs arrive from a biodynamic farm just a few minutes away. Peaches from

Dry Creek Valley are picked at their peak of juiciness. The arugula is still moist from the morning dew. When you are so close to the product, everything simply tastes better, particularly when served with Sonoma County wines.

> **"** I love living in Sonoma County because it makes my chef's job easy. When you start with such wonderful ingredients, and have world-class wineries as your neighbors, you simply must gather with friends, put together a meal and revel in the goodness that each season brings. **"**

I moved away from Sonoma County for a few years to expand my culinary knowledge, and realized how spoiled I had become by our region's endless variety of fresh meats, seafood and produce. I had taken for granted that green beans were always sweet, and that fish was so fresh it could be used for sashimi. I knew I had to move back to Sonoma County when the tomatoes available to me were tasteless—picked while green and unripe, so that they could withstand being shipped hundreds of miles.

The chefs who contributed recipes to this book feel as fortunate as I do to live and work here. We hope you enjoy the dishes, visit the wineries, restaurants and lodgings, and taste for yourself the bounty of Sonoma County.

recipes
from the wineries & lodgings

brunch

Applewood Inn & Restaurant

13555 highway 116, guerneville, ca 95446
707-869-9093

www.applewoodinn.com

(This recipe is an adaptation of one published in Relish Magazine, which awarded a stay at Applewood Inn as the grand prize in the magazine's Sunny Side Up Sweepstakes in March 2008. The dish takes advantage of the abundance of ripe heirloom tomatoes and fresh herbs that grow in our 2-acre organic kitchen garden every summer. **Serves 4**)

italian tomato fritters

chef **Jim Caron**

ingredients

4 tablespoons olive oil
1 pound Italian hot sausage, diced
1 yellow onion, chopped
4 garlic cloves, minced
2 teaspoons fresh oregano, chopped
2 teaspoons fresh basil, chopped
½ pound ripe red tomatoes, chopped
¾ cup all-purpose flour
4 large eggs, beaten
salt and black pepper to taste
½ cup crème fraiche
2 to 3 tablespoons green onions, chopped

directions

In a large saucepan over medium-high heat, heat 1 tablespoon of the oil and sauté the sausage until it just starts to turn brown. Add the onions and cook until they're translucent and soft. Add the garlic, oregano, basil and tomatoes. Reduce the heat and cook slowly until well combined, about 10 minutes. Set aside to cool.

When the mixture is cool, add the flour and the eggs, and mix until well blended. Season with salt and pepper.

Place a large skillet over medium heat and coat the pan with the remaining 3 tablespoons of oil. When the oil is hot, drop 8 large spoonfuls of the batter into the skillet, and press each one down with a spatula. Cook the fritters until they're golden brown on one side, about 4 minutes. Flip the fritters and cook the other side until golden brown, about 3 minutes.

To serve, put two fritters on each of four plates and top each with a dollop of crème fraiche. Garnish with the chopped green onions.

Avalon Luxury B & B

11910 graton road, sebastopol, ca 95472
707-824-0880

www.avalonluxuryinn.com

This is one of our most popular recipes at Avalon. When we first started, our specialty was buttermilk pancakes served with good ol' organic maple syrup. It was a comfortable favorite, yet we wanted to spice things up a bit and added bananas. The pancakes were delicious, but then we had a problem because the flavor of the syrup didn't enhance the flavor of the pancakes. The hunt began for the perfect syrup, and when we couldn't find one, I created my own Spiced Syrup, which complements the pancakes perfectly. The nuts add a hearty crunch and another layer of flavor. We serve these pancakes with organic chicken-apple sausages. **Serves 4**

banana nut pancakes

with spiced syrup

chef Hilary McCalla

ingredients

Syrup

½ cup granulated sugar
1 tablespoon cornstarch
1-½ teaspoons ground cinnamon
½ teaspoon ground nutmeg
½ teaspoon salt
½ cup water
3 tablespoons fresh lemon juice
1 teaspoon vanilla extract
2 tablespoons butter

Pancakes

1 ripe banana, mashed
1 egg
1-¼ cups buttermilk
2 tablespoons safflower oil (or any light, flavorless oil)
1-¼ cups all-purpose flour
1-½ teaspoons baking powder
½ teaspoon baking soda
½ teaspoon salt
1 cup pecans or walnuts, coarsely chopped

directions

To prepare the syrup, in a medium saucepan, stir together the sugar, cornstarch, cinnamon, nutmeg and salt until the mixture is well-blended, with absolutely no lumps of cornstarch remaining. Add the water and the lemon juice and cook, stirring constantly, over medium heat. When the syrup boils, it will thicken and clarify slightly. Remove the syrup from the heat and add the vanilla and butter. Keep stirring until the butter is melted and blended in.

To prepare the pancakes, in a large mixing bowl, combine the banana, egg, buttermilk and oil. In a medium bowl, combine the flour, baking powder, baking soda and salt.

Heat a griddle over medium heat until it's evenly heated. Add the dry ingredients to the wet ingredients in the large bowl and stir until just blended. The batter will be lumpy. Gently stir in the nuts.

Oil the griddle (if necessary). Drop the batter by ⅓ cupfuls onto the hot griddle. When bubbles form on top of the pancakes, flip them over and cook the other side. The pancakes are done when both sides are golden in color. Serve with the syrup on the side.

Belle de Jour Inn

16276 healdsburg avenue, healdsburg, ca 95448
707-431-9777

www.belledejourinn.com

Seafood makes for a protein-rich breakfast to get you started on the day. Assemble this dish the night before, put it in the refrigerator, and bake it the next morning. Easy! **Serves 8 to 10**

brunch scallops

chef Brenda Hearn, Innkeeper

ingredients

1 tablespoon butter for the baking pan
3 cups stale bread or croissant cubes
1 pound fresh bay scallops
12 large eggs
½ cup heavy cream
1 teaspoon kosher salt
½ teaspoon white pepper
10 ounces cheddar cheese, shredded
2 teaspoons Aleppo pepper, crushed, or paprika

directions

Coat a 9x12 baking pan with butter. Spread the cubed bread or croissants in the pan, then distribute the scallops evenly among the bread cubes.

In a large bowl, whisk the eggs, cream, salt and pepper together. Pour the mixture over the bread and scallops. Sprinkle the cheese over the top, then sprinkle the Aleppo pepper or paprika. Cover the pan tightly with plastic wrap and refrigerate it overnight.

The next morning, preheat the oven to 350°. Bake the scallop casserole for 30 minutes. Remove it from the oven, adjust the rack on the broiler to 6 inches from the heat, and heat the broiler. Broil the casserole for 5 minutes and serve immediately.

pair with sauvignon blanc or pinot blanc

Calderwood Inn

25 west grant street, healdsburg, ca 95448
707-431-1110

www.calderwoodinn.com

These tender, flaky scones are a staple at Calderwood Inn. We like to serve them hot from the oven, with lemon curd, blackberry jam and sweet butter. You can prepare the scones in advance and freeze them for future baking. **Makes 12 scones**

lemon
buttermilk scones

chef Susan Moreno, Innkeeper

ingredients

2 cups all-purpose flour
¼ cup granulated sugar
2 tablespoons baking powder
½ teaspoon baking soda
¼ teaspoon salt
zest of 1 lemon, grated
1 stick (4 ounces) very cold butter, cut into 16 pieces
½ cup cold buttermilk
1 egg
2 tablespoons clear decorator sugar crystals

directions preheat oven to 425°

In the bowl of a food processor, mix the dry ingredients and the lemon zest. Add the cold butter pieces and pulse until the butter is in coarse bits (about 5 pulses). Do not overmix, as the butter will get warm and the scones will be tough.

In a small mixing bowl, beat the buttermilk and the egg together. With the food processor running, add the buttermilk/egg mixture to the dry ingredients. Mix only until the contents ball up and pull away from the sides of the processor bowl; do not overmix.

Remove the batter from the bowl and place it on a lightly floured work surface. The batter will be sticky. Dust the top of the dough lightly with flour, and using a pastry scraper, gently turn the dough twice to knead. Form the dough into a flat disk and pat it to about 9 inches wide and ½-inch thick. Sprinkle the sugar crystals over the top, gently pressing them into the dough. Using the pastry scraper dipped in flour, divide the disk into 12 wedges. Place the wedges onto a large baking sheet lined with parchment paper.

At this point you can freeze the scones for baking later. Place the baking sheet with the scones in the freezer, uncovered; once frozen, remove them from the sheet and place them in an airtight bag, then store in the freezer. If you plan to bake the scones right away but need to hold them for a few minutes, place the baking sheet in the refrigerator to keep the dough cold.

Bake the scones for 12 to 15 minutes, or until the tops just begin to brown. If the scones are frozen, bake them for an additional 2 minutes or until done.

Camellia Inn

211 north street, healdsburg, ca 95448
707-433-8182

www.camelliainn.com

This recipe was a favorite of Delmas (Del) Lewand, who opened
and operated the Camellia Inn with her husband, Ray, in the 1980s.
Del, who loved to cook and entertain, ran the inn for more than
25 years. This is an excellent brunch entrée and also works well
as a light lunch when accompanied by a dressed green salad.
Lucy Lewand, the current owner/innkeeper, has kept her mother's
recipes to share with guests, to honor Del's memory and the
guests who have been coming to the inn for years. **Serves 4**

galette

with smoked salmon and potato
chef Lucy Lewand, Innkeeper

ingredients

2 teaspoons olive oil
1 cup onion, sliced
2 to 3 white potatoes, peeled
1 9x9 sheet of frozen puff pastry, thawed
2 tablespoons whipping cream
1 teaspoon dried dill weed
salt and pepper to taste
1 tablespoon capers, drained
4 ounces smoked salmon, thinly sliced
1 pint sour cream

directions preheat oven to 350°

Heat the oil in a 10- to 12-inch frying pan. When the oil is hot, add the onion slices and cook them until they're limp but not brown. Let them cool. Thinly slice the potatoes crosswise.

Lay the puff pastry out flat on a lightly floured board. Trim off the corners of the pastry to form a circle and, with a floured rolling pin, roll out the pastry to form an 11- to 12-inch circle. Transfer the circle to a baking sheet.

Spread the onions onto the dough, leaving a 2-inch border. Sprinkle the onions with salt and pepper. Arrange the potato slices, slightly overlapping, over the onions, and sprinkle again with salt, pepper and the dill weed. Fold the edges of the dough over the potatoes. Drizzle the cream over the potatoes and bake for about 35 minutes, rotating the pan if necessary, until the crust is brown and the potatoes tender. Top the galette with the capers and arrange the sliced salmon over all, while the galette is still warm. Serve with sour cream on the side.

pair with camellia cellars first kiss

Case Ranch Inn

7446 poplar drive, forestville, ca 95436
707-887-8711

www.caseranchinn.com

Prior to becoming B&B owners, we served this recipe at many family gatherings. Our guests consistently praise this frittata and we love it because it is so simple to prepare. It tastes great accompanied by roasted potatoes and sausage. **Serves 8 to 10**

Frittata

with spinach and mushroom

chef Diana Van Ry, Innkeeper

ingredients

½ to ¾ pound white mushrooms, sliced
2 tablespoons olive oil
1 10-ounce package of chopped frozen spinach, thawed and drained
½ cup all-purpose flour
1 teaspoon baking powder
10 large eggs, lightly beaten
3 tablespoons vegetable oil
2 cups small-curd cottage cheese
¼ pound pepper jack cheese, grated
¼ pound Monterey Jack cheese, grated

directions preheat oven to 350°

In a large frying pan over medium heat, warm the olive oil and sauté the mushrooms until their moisture has been released and they're rather dry. Add the spinach and stir 1 to 2 minutes to warm up the spinach with the mushrooms. Remove the pan from the heat and set aside to cool.

Butter or lightly oil a 9x13 shallow baking dish. In a large bowl, mix the flour and baking powder. Add the eggs and the vegetable oil, blending well. Blend in the mushroom/spinach mixture and the three cheeses.

Put the mixture in the prepared baking dish and bake for 45 minutes to 1 hour, or until set. Check for doneness by inserting a knife or toothpick into the center of the frittata; the knife or toothpick should come out dry. Let the frittata stand for 5 minutes, then cut into squares and serve hot.

Creekside Inn & Resort

16180 neeley road, guerneville, ca 95446
707-869-3623

www.creeksideinn.com

We are always looking for new ways to serve eggs, particularly in dishes that hold up well for late arrivals for breakfast. We think this dish tastes like it's a lot more trouble to make than it really is. Prepare the pesto and fry the basil leaves before starting on the eggs. If you don't want to fry the basil, substitute minced chives instead. The pesto is great with asparagus and artichokes, too. **Makes 12 egg wontons**

wonton huevos

with roasted red pepper and macadamia pesto

chef Lynn Crescione, Innkeeper

ingredients

Roasted Red Pepper and Macadamia Pesto

2 roasted red bell peppers, peeled and seeded
1 cup macadamia nuts, chopped
2 large or 4 small cloves of garlic
2 tablespoons olive oil
¼ to ½ teaspoon bottled red pepper sauce
Salt to taste

Wonton Huevos

24 square wonton wrappers
1 stick (4 ounces) butter, melted
12 teaspoons feta cheese
12 eggs
12 teaspoons of roasted red pepper and
    macadamia pesto (see recipe)
3 medium tomatoes, quartered (optional)

Fried Basil Leaves

1 bunch fresh basil
1 cup canola oil

directions preheat oven to 350°

To prepare the pesto, place the roasted peppers, macadamia nuts and garlic in a blender or food processor. Blend until almost smooth, while drizzling in the olive oil. Add the pepper sauce and salt to taste. Set aside.

To prepare the fried basil leaves, pull 24 leaves from the bunch of basil, and wash and thoroughly dry them. Pour the canola oil in a frying pan and place the pan over medium-high heat. Carefully drop the leaves into the hot oil and fry them until their color lightens and their edges start to turn slightly brown. Skim off the leaves and allow them to drain on paper towels.

To prepare the egg wontons, butter a 12-muffin tin. Line each cup with 1 wonton wrapper, brush the wrapper with melted butter, and top with another wrapper. Brush again with melted butter, and put the tin in the preheated oven for 10 minutes.

Remove the tin from the oven and place a teaspoon of feta in each baked wrapper, followed by 1 whole, cracked egg. Place a teaspoon of pesto on top of each egg.

Return the tin to the oven for 5 to 7 minutes, or until the eggs are barely set. Remove the muffin tin and allow the eggs to cool slightly. Carefully remove the wonton eggs from the tin, place 1 or 2 on each plate, and top each with 2 fried basil leaves (minced chives are a suitable replacement). Serve the eggs warm or at room temperature, accompanied by optional tomato wedges.

pair with harvest moon russian river valley sparkling gewurztraminer brut

Farmhouse Inn & Restaurant

7871 river road, forestville, ca 95436
707-887-3300

www.farmhouseinn.com

Our talented breakfast chef, Reyna Levaro, regularly earns kudos for this recipe, which is simple to make at home yet complex in flavor. Reyna started cooking for her family at a young age and had her own restaurant and bakery in Mexico. She moved to the United States in 1996, and in 2002, she joined Farmhouse Inn & Restaurant. Reyna enjoys cooking with fresh, seasonal products, yet her Spinach-Cheddar Egg Bake can be made year-round. **Serves 6**

spinach-cheddar

egg bake

chef Reyna Levaro

ingredients

1 bag fresh spinach, cooked, squeezed dry and chopped
16 ounces cottage cheese
1 bunch green onions, chopped
¼ teaspoon salt
¼ teaspoon black pepper
½ cup flour
3 tablespoons fresh dill, chopped, or 1 tablespoon dill weed
1 cup sharp cheddar cheese, grated
8 eggs

directions preheat oven to 375°

In a large bowl, thoroughly mix the spinach, cottage cheese, green onions, salt, pepper, flour, dill and half of the cheddar cheese.

Grease a 9x11 baking dish. Spread the mixture in the pan. Beat the eggs and pour them over the mixture. Bake for about 45 minutes. Sprinkle the remaining half-cup of cheddar cheese on the top of the dish and bake for 15 minutes more.

pair with your favorite sparkling wine

George Alexander House

423 matheson street, healdsburg, ca 95448
707-433-1358

www.georgealexanderhouse.com

We have a very productive pear tree in our backyard. A couple
of years ago, we had hundreds of delicious pears from that tree,
and I needed some new recipes for our guests. I searched the
Internet for ideas, and after combining a few ingredients, came
up with this delicious brunch dish. **Serves 12**

brunch

pear walnut squares

chef Holly Schatz, Innkeeper

ingredients

1-¾ cups flour
¾ cup powdered sugar
¾ cup butter, softened
1 teaspoon cinnamon, divided
¼ teaspoon salt
½ cup walnuts, chopped
3 ripe Bartlett pears, peeled, cored and sliced
3 large eggs
1/3 cup brown sugar, packed
1-½ teaspoons vanilla extract

directions preheat oven to 350°

In a medium bowl, combine the flour, powdered sugar, butter, ½ teaspoon of the cinnamon and the salt. Mix well.

Press the mixture into the bottom of a greased 7x11 baking dish. Top with the nuts and pear slices. Beat together the eggs, brown sugar, vanilla and the remaining cinnamon until well combined. Pour over the pears and bake for 35 to 40 minutes, until the mixture is set in the center. Cool completely before cutting into squares.

pair with sauvignon blanc

Haydon Street Inn

321 haydon street, healdsburg, ca 95448
707-433-5228

www.haydon.com

John Harasty and Keren Colsten purchased Haydon Street Inn in May 2006, fulfilling a dream to own their own business and live in Sonoma County. John was the executive chef at Churchill Downs racetrack in Louisville for 12 years and has cooked for Ronald Reagan, Burt Reynolds, Goldie Hawn, Rodney Dangerfield, Yul Brynner, Ozzy Osbourne and other celebrities. John and Keren advise those who prepare these fruit-studded scones to not overmix the dough; overly energetic mixing can lead to a less tender scone. **Serves 8**

brunch

cream scones

chefs John Harasty and Keren Colsten, Innkeepers

ingredients

Scones

2-½ cups all-purpose flour
3 tablespoons granulated sugar
2-½ teaspoons baking powder
½ teaspoon salt
½ cup cold, unsalted butter, cut into 8 pieces
⅓ cup dried cranberries or dried apricots, diced
2 lemons, grated zest only
1 egg
1 cup half and half
½ teaspoon vanilla extract

Egg Wash

1 tablespoon water
1 egg
2 tablespoons coarse white sugar or turbinado sugar

directions preheat oven to 375°

To prepare the scones, line a baking sheet with parchment paper. In a large bowl, stir together the flour, granulated sugar, baking powder and salt. Cut the cold butter pieces into the flour mixture, until the pieces are pea-sized. Stir in the dried fruit and lemon zest.

In a small bowl, beat the egg slightly with a fork. Stir in the half and half and vanilla. Pour the cream mixture all at once into the flour mixture, stirring with a fork to form a soft dough. Do not overmix.

Turn the dough out onto a lightly floured pastry cloth or board, and knead a few times until the dough is smooth. Flecks of butter should still be visible. Roll or pat the dough into a round about ¾-inch thick. Use a biscuit cutter to cut out 8 rounds of dough, or use a sharp knife or pizza cutter to cut out 8 wedges. Separate the dough shapes and place them on the prepared baking sheet.

To prepare the egg wash, in a small bowl, beat the egg and water. Brush the mixture over the top of the scones and sprinkle them with the coarse or turbinado sugar. Bake the scones for 15 to 17 minutes, until they are puffed and golden brown, and a cake tester inserted in the center comes out clean.

Highlands Resort

14000 woodland drive, guerneville, ca 95446
707-869-0333

www.highlandsresort.com

Hey, we live in Northern California and wear Birkenstocks, so what else would we call this tasty granola? Homemade granola has been the star of the California continental breakfast we've served at the Highlands Resort for more than 10 years. When chef Lynette McLean and her husband, Ken, bought the resort, they tested various recipes until they found that the very best granola was the one created by Lynette's mother, Kathleen Sommers. Kathleen has made the recipe for her family since the early 1970s and today, her children bake their own granola, too. **Serves 6 to 9**

granola nirvana

chef Lynette McLean, Innkeeper

ingredients

6 cups rolled oats (not quick-cooking)
2 cups oat bran
1 cup sweetened, flaked coconut
½ cup sesame seeds
²/₃ cup vegetable oil
½ cup honey
1 tablespoon vanilla extract
1 cup almonds, slivered
1 cup raisins or dried cranberries

directions preheat oven to 250°

In a large bowl, combine the rolled oats, oat bran, coconut and sesame seeds. In a small bowl, combine the vegetable oil, honey and vanilla extract, and add to the dry mixture. Stir well. Pour the combined mixture onto a baking sheet (with sides) and spread out the granola in an even layer.

Bake the granola for 1 hour, stirring every 20 minutes to avoid burning. The granola is done when the coconut and oats are a light golden color. Cool the granola, then add the almonds and raisins or dried cranberries. Store the granola tightly covered; it can also be frozen in resealable freezer bags. Serve the granola the traditional way, in a bowl with milk, or layer it in a wine glass with plain yogurt and fresh berries, parfait-style. Pair with milk!

Honor Mansion

14891 grove street, healdsburg, ca 95448
707-433-4277

www.honormansion.com

We created this dish after we realized that we had many guests who enjoyed a glass of sparkling wine, Chardonnay or Sauvignon Blanc with their breakfast. This recipe, which is complementary to most dry white wines, was featured in "The National Culinary Review." **Serves 6**

santa fe bake

chef Cathi Fowler, Innkeeper

ingredients

Santa Fe Bake

non-stick spray
12 eggs
¾ quart heavy cream
1 onion, diced
2 whole red bell peppers, diced
dash Tabasco sauce
1 cup Monterey Jack cheese, shredded
1 cup cheddar cheese, shredded
sour cream, for garnish
tomato for garnish, sliced
red, green and yellow bell peppers for garnish, diced

Sun-Dried Tomato Sauce

1 15-ounce can tomato sauce
1 cup heavy cream
1 cup sour cream
¾ tablespoon vegetable base
1 tablespoon sugar
2 tablespoons sun-dried tomatoes, chopped
½ cup fresh tomatoes, diced
12 small tomato wedges, for garnish

directions preheat oven to 350°

Coat a 9x13 baking pan with non-stick spray.

To prepare the Santa Fe Bake, in a large bowl, mix together the eggs and heavy cream. Add the onion, red peppers, Tabasco sauce and one-half of each of the two cheeses. Stir the ingredients together and mix well. Pour the mixture into the pan and cover with the remaining cheeses.

Bake for about 1 hour, or until a knife inserted in the center comes out clean. Remove the pan from the oven and let the dish cool for at least 10 minutes.

To prepare the sun-dried tomato sauce, in a large saucepan, add the tomato sauce, heavy cream, ½ cup of the sour cream, vegetable base, sugar, sun-dried tomatoes and diced fresh tomatoes, and heat through.

To serve, cut the Santa Fe Bake into 6 squares. Spoon the sauce onto each of 6 plates and place a square on each. Top each square with more sauce, a dollop of the remaining sour cream, a tomato slice and a sprinkling of the multi-colored diced peppers.

pair with passalacqua chardonnay or mauritson sauvignon blanc

Hope-Merrill House

21253 geyserville avenue, geyserville, ca 95441
707-857-3356

www.hope-inns.com

Decadent describes this coffee cake bursting with
blueberries and crunchy walnuts. Sour cream
gives the cake a rich, smooth texture. **Serves 8-10**

sour cream coffee cake

with blueberries and walnuts

chef Cosette Scheiber, Innkeeper

ingredients

½ cup unsalted butter
1 cup sugar
2 eggs
2 cups all-purpose flour, sifted
1 teaspoon baking soda
½ teaspoon salt
1 cup sour cream
¼ cup sugar
1 teaspoon cinnamon, ground
1 teaspoon vanilla extract
1 cup fresh or frozen blueberries (thawed)
½ cup walnuts

directions preheat oven to 350°

Grease a Bundt pan. In a large bowl, cream the butter with the 1 cup of sugar. Mix in the eggs. Sift the flour, baking soda and salt together and add to the egg mixture, alternating with the sour cream. Pour half of the batter into the prepared pan and spread it evenly.

In a small bowl, combine the remaining ¼ cup of sugar, cinnamon and vanilla. Spread half of this mixture onto the first layer of batter, then sprinkle the blueberries and walnuts over the top. Spread the remaining batter in the pan, and top with the remaining sugar/cinnamon mixture. Bake for 50 to 60 minutes, or until a toothpick inserted in the center comes out clean. Slice into 2-inch segments and serve.

Jenner Inn & Cottages

10400 coast highway one, jenner, ca 95450
707-865-2377

www.jennerinn.com

Our manager, Christine Calloway-Holt, formerly managed the 575-year-old Borthwick Castle outside of Edinburgh, Scotland, where Mary Queen of Scots once slept. Christine brought this recipe with her to Jenner Inn & Cottages, and our guests love the buttery richness of these cookies. The recipe is simple, although it's imperative to cut the cookies into their finger-sized shapes as soon as they come out of the oven. **Makes 50 cookies**

orange shortbread

chef **Christine Calloway-Holt**

ingredients

2-½ pounds flour
12 ounces cornstarch
12 ounces superfine sugar
1 teaspoon salt
2 oranges, finely grated zest only
2 pounds unsalted butter, softened

directions preheat oven to 350°

Sift together the flour and cornstarch and place in a large bowl. Add the sugar, salt and orange zest, then mix in the butter by hand, rubbing the mixture until it has the texture of bread crumbs.

Line a 12x17 baking sheet (with sides) with parchment paper. Firmly push the dough onto the baking sheet, using your hands, and level so that the surface is as flat and even as possible. Refrigerate the dough until it gets firm.

Remove the shortbread from the refrigerator and with a fork, punch holes over the surface of the dough. Bake for approximately 30 minutes, or until the cookies just start to take on a tinge of gold. The shortbread is done when a needle inserted into the center comes out clean. It's important not to overbake the shortbread, as this will dry out the butter.

Remove the baking sheet from the oven and immediately cut the cookies into finger-shaped rectangles, approximately 1 inch wide and 3 inches long. Dust with superfine sugar and leave the shortbread in the tray to cool. Gently remove the cookies from the pan and store in an air-tight container.

pair with english or scottish breakfast tea

Old Crocker Inn B & B

1126 old crocker inn road, cloverdale, ca 95425
707-894-4000

www.oldcrockerinn.com

We always have something sweet on the sideboard for our guests to enjoy. This cake is probably our most popular treat, especially when it's just come out of the oven. Many of our guests sneak over for a second and third piece when no one is looking. **Serves 10 to 12**

fresh apple cake

chef **Marcia Babb**

ingredients

2 cups plus 1 tablespoon sugar
1 tablespoon plus 1 teaspoon cinnamon
3 eggs, beaten
4 cups unpeeled apples, cored and chopped into small dice
1 cup canola or vegetable oil
2 cups all-purpose flour
2 cups plus 1 tablespoon sugar
1 teaspoon salt
1-½ teaspoons baking soda
powered sugar (optional)

directions preheat oven to 350°

Grease a 9-inch Bundt pan. In a small bowl, combine 1 tablespoon of sugar and 1 tablespoon of cinnamon, and coat the greased pan with the mixture.

In a large bowl, combine the eggs and oil and mix well by hand. Stir in the chopped apples. In another bowl, whisk together the flour, remaining 2 cups of sugar, salt, baking soda and remaining 1 teaspoon of cinnamon. Stir the flour mixture into the apples, until just combined.

Spoon the batter into the pan and bake for approximately 1 hour. To serve, let the cake cool slightly, then cut it into 10 to 12 slices. If desired, sift powdered sugar over the top of the cooled cake, then slice.

pair with viognier

The Raford Inn of Healdsburg

10630 wohler road, healdsburg, ca 95448
707-887-9573

www.rafordinn.com

This frittata is simple to prepare, colorful, and a huge hit with our guests. I serve it with bacon or sausage, scones and fresh fruit. Look for sun-dried tomato pesto and fresh bruschetta sauce in the refrigerated section of your favorite grocery store. **Serves 4 to 6**

mediterranean frittata

chef Rita Wells, Innkeeper

ingredients

8 large eggs
¼ teaspoon salt
¼ teaspoon black pepper
2 cups artichoke hearts, quartered
½ cup black olives, sliced
½ cup feta cheese, crumbled
3 tablespoons sun-dried tomato pesto
fresh bruschetta sauce with basil

directions preheat oven to 350°

Coat a 9-inch glass pie plate with non-stick cooking spray. In a medium bowl, whisk together the eggs, salt and pepper, and pour the mixture into the pie plate.

Sprinkle the artichoke hearts, olives and feta cheese on top of the eggs and gently mix them in. Add small dollops of the pesto all over the egg mixture, pressing the pesto in lightly with a spoon. Bake for 45 minutes.

To serve, cut the frittata into 4 to 6 wedges and top each with the bruschetta sauce.

pair with sparkling wine

Rued Vineyards & Winery

3850 dry creek road, healdsburg, ca 95448
707-433-3261

www.ruedvineyards.com

This recipe calls for heirloom apples; Golden Delicious are a fine choice, or try a combination of Granny Smith and Pippin apples. All three varieties are readily available in grocery stores. **Serves 8**

golden heirloom
apple strata

chef Greg Barnes, Simply Good Food

ingredients

1-½ cups heirloom apples, peeled, cored and cubed
1 day-old French bread loaf, or 4 to 5 large croissants, cubed
8 ounces cold cream cheese, diced
1 cup golden raisins
10 eggs
2-½ cups half and half
1 stick (4 ounces) butter, melted
1 teaspoon nutmeg
1 teaspoon cinnamon
1 teaspoon fresh lemon thyme, chopped (optional)
4 tablespoons sugar
1 ounce Calvados or other brandy

directions preheat oven to 350°

Butter a 9x13 casserole dish. Arrange the apples, bread, cream cheese and raisins in the bottom, spreading evenly.

In a large bowl, combine the eggs, half and half, melted butter, nutmeg, cinnamon, lemon thyme (if using), sugar and brandy. Pour the mixture over the apple mixture, cover the dish in plastic wrap, and refrigerate for 2 to 6 hours.

Remove the casserole from the refrigerator and remove the plastic wrap. Sprinkle the top of the strata with sugar and bake in the center of the oven for 45 to 50 minutes, or until golden brown. Allow to cool for a few minutes before serving.

pair with rued russian river valley chardonnay

Santa Nella House B & B

12130 highway 116, guerneville, ca 95446
707-869-9488

www.santanellahouse.com

These pancakes are so light, you'll need a fork to hold
them down on your plate! If you have access to fresh
blackberries, make your own blackberry syrup—it's
far superior to the store-bought kind. **Serves 6**

ricotta pancakes

with blackberry syrup

chefs Bob Reeves and Betsy Taggart

ingredients

Blackberry Syrup

1-½ cups sugar
¾ cup water
2-¼ cups fresh blackberries

Pancakes

3 eggs
1 teaspoon baking powder
1 pinch salt
zest from 1 lemon
½-pound whole-milk ricotta cheese
²/₃ cup whole milk
½ cup flour

directions

To prepare the blackberry syrup, in a medium saucepan, add the sugar and water. Over medium heat, stir the mixture until the sugar is dissolved. Turn the heat to high and bring the mixture to a boil. Boil, uncovered and without stirring, for 5 minutes. Let this "simple syrup" cool.

Puree 1-½ cups of the blackberries in a blender or food processor and pour into a mixing bowl. Add ½ cup of the simple syrup and mix well. Taste to determine if you need more syrup (tart berries may need more sweetness). Chop the remaining ¾ cup of blackberries and fold them into the bowl. Gently warm the syrup before serving.

To prepare the pancakes, separate the egg yolks from the whites. In a stainless steel mixing bowl, whip the egg whites until they're stiff, then set them aside. In a separate bowl, mix the rest of the ingredients, and fold in the egg whites.

Heat a griddle coated with shortening. Ladle one spoonful of batter onto the hot griddle and cook until bubbles appear on the surface of the pancake. Flip the pancake and continue cooking until the underside is golden brown. Serve immediately with blackberry syrup and butter.

pair with korbel moscoto frizzante

The Shelford House Inn

29955 river road, cloverdale, ca 95425
800-833-6479

www.shelford.com

These scones are one of our guests' favorites, and we serve them every year for our Victorian Mother's Day Tea. We use our antique teapots, cups and saucers, and offer everyone a mimosa—orange juice and sparkling wine—in lovely crystal Champagne glasses. **Serves 8**

cranberry scones

with devonshire cream

chef Anna Smith

ingredients

Scones

2 cups all-purpose flour
¼ cup sugar, plus more for sprinkling on top
¼ teaspoon salt
2 teaspoons baking powder
½ teaspoon baking soda
½ cup cold butter, cut into small pieces
½ cup dried cranberries
1 large egg
½ cup buttermilk

Devonshire Cream

5 ounces cream cheese, softened at room temperature
1 cup heavy cream
½ cup powdered sugar

directions preheat oven to 425°

To prepare the Devonshire cream, in a medium mixing bowl, add all three ingredients and whip until blended. This yields approximately 2 cups.

To prepare the scones, in a large mixing bowl, combine the flour, ¼ cup sugar, salt, baking powder and baking soda. Add the butter pieces and cut them in by hand with a pastry blender. Stir in the cranberries.

In a separate bowl, whisk together the egg and buttermilk. Add the egg mixture to the flour mixture and stir with a fork, until the ingredients are moistened and hold together. Gather the dough into a ball and transfer it to a lightly floured work surface; knead several times.

Pat the dough into an 8-inch round. Sprinkle the dough with sugar, and with a sharp knife, cut the round into 8 same-sized wedges. Place the wedges slightly apart on an ungreased baking sheet and bake until golden brown, about 12 minutes. Serve immediately with Devonshire cream on the side.

pair with sparkling mimosas

Sonoma Orchid Inn

12850 river road, guerneville, ca 95446
707-887-1033

www.sonomaorchidinn.com

We first used this recipe from Marion Cunningham's "The Breakfast Book" last year and our guests raved about it. We modified the recipe slightly and always have good results with our own farm-fresh eggs. This is a surprisingly good way to eat oatmeal—like a large, fluffy oatmeal cookie. **Serves 4 to 6**

oatmeal soufflé

ingredients

granulated sugar, for sprinkling
1 cup milk
2 tablespoons butter
¾ cup quick-cooking oats
⅓ cup cream cheese
¼ teaspoon salt
½ cup brown sugar
½ teaspoon nutmeg
½ teaspoon cinnamon
4 eggs, yolks separated
½ cup raisins or dried blueberries
½ cup walnuts, chopped

directions preheat oven to 325°

Butter a 1-½-quart soufflé or casserole dish and sprinkle the dish with sugar. In a small saucepan, add the milk and butter and heat until barely boiling. Slowly add the oats, stirring constantly. Cook the oat mixture until it's thick, stirring often.

Remove the oats from the heat and add the cream cheese, salt, brown sugar, nutmeg and cinnamon. Stir briskly to blend. In a separate bowl, beat the egg yolks slightly and slowly add them to the oatmeal, stirring constantly. Stir in the raisins (or dried blueberries) and walnuts.

Beat the egg whites until they are stiff yet still moist. Using a rubber spatula, gently stir and fold the egg whites into the oatmeal mixture. Fold only until no large lumps of whites remain, and no more. Spoon the mixture into the soufflé dish and bake for 35 to 40 minutes, or until the center still trembles a trifle, yet most of the soufflé is set. Serve immediately, with cream or warm milk, although this soufflé is still tasty when cold and fallen.

appetizers

Fern Grove Cottages

16650 highway 116, guerneville, ca 95446
888-243-2674

www.ferngrove.com

This is a dandy dipping sauce for breadsticks, sliced and toasted French bread, celery sticks and just about any other crisp vegetables. It's also a lively addition when drizzled over pork tenderloin and chicken tenders. **Serves 8 as an appetizer**

michael's
ginger dipping sauce

chef Mike Kennett

ingredients

2 tablespoons butter
2 green onions, including tops, finely chopped
½ teaspoon fresh ginger, minced
3 tablespoons mango-based chutney
⅓ cup Marsala wine
¾ cup chicken broth
¾ cup whipping cream
1 tablespoon crystallized ginger, chopped

directions

In a frying pan, melt the butter over medium heat. Add the onions, fresh ginger, chutney, Marsala and chicken broth and stir. Increase the heat and continue to stir until the mixture is reduced by half. Add the whipping cream and bring to boil. Stir until the mixture is reduced to 1-½ cups.

Pour the sauce into a serving bowl, sprinkle with the chopped crystallized ginger and serve warm.

pair with fume blanc, sauvignon blanc or dry gewurztraminer

Hanna Winery

9280 highway 128, healdsburg, ca 95448
707-431-4310

5353 occidental road, santa rosa, ca 95401
707-575-3371

www.hannawinery.com

Muhammarah is a dish from Aleppo, a town in northern Syria that is famous for its hot and sweet hybrid peppers. We substitute local sweet red peppers and any kind of hot peppers for the Aleppo peppers. The color of this spread is a gorgeous brick red. Look for the tart and only slightly sweet pomegranate molasses in Mediterranean and Asian markets. I like the smoky taste imparted by cooking the peppers on the grill, but you can also roast them in the oven with very good results. **Serves 6**

muhammarah dip

chef Chris Hanna

ingredients

2-½ pounds sweet red peppers
1 or 2 small hot chiles, such as hot Hungarian or jalapeno
1-½ cups walnuts, shelled
½ cup stoned wheat crackers
1 tablespoon fresh lemon juice
2 tablespoons pomegranate molasses
½ teaspoon cumin, ground
salt and pepper to taste
2 tablespoons olive oil
1 tablespoon chopped parsley

directions preheat a grill

Roast the red peppers and the chiles on a hot grill, turning frequently, until the skins are blistered all over. Place the peppers in a covered bowl or paper bag and let them cool. Remove the skin, seeds and membranes.

In a food processor, grind the walnuts, crackers, lemon juice, pomegranate molasses, cumin, salt and pepper until the mixture is smooth. Add the peppers and puree until creamy. With the blades running, add the olive oil in a thin stream. Adjust the seasoning with salt and pepper.

Place the spread in a small serving dish, drizzle olive oil over the top, and garnish with the chopped parsley. Serve with pita triangles or thin-sliced French bread.

pair with hanna russian river valley sauvignon blanc and pinot noir

Huntington Wine Cellars

53 front street, healdsburg, ca 95448
707-433-5215

www.huntingtonwine.com

These are great party snacks, and the meatballs can be made one day ahead; bake them the next day. Harissa, a spicy red pepper paste, and pomegranate molasses can be found in most large supermarkets and specialty grocery stores. **Serves 6**

appetizers

harissa chicken meatballs

with pomegranate barbecue glaze

chef Mark Stark, Willi's Wine Bar and Willi's Seafood & Raw Bar

ingredients

Pomegranate Barbecue Sauce

½ tablespoon coriander seed
½ tablespoon red pepper flakes
½ tablespoon cumin seed
2 tablespoons olive oil
½ cup shallots, sliced
1-½ tablespoons garlic, chopped
1 quart molasses
5 ounces pomegranate molasses

Meatballs

2 tablespoons olive oil
1 onion, diced
2 cloves garlic, minced
½ tablespoon harissa
1 teaspoon cinnamon, ground
½ teaspoon cumin, ground
1/8 teaspoon cayenne pepper
¼ teaspoon saffron
1 tablespoon cilantro, chopped
2 pounds ground chicken
1 egg

directions preheat oven to 450°

To prepare the pomegranate sauce, in a medium saucepan, lightly toast the coriander seed, red pepper flakes and cumin seed over medium heat until fragrant. Add the olive oil, shallots and garlic and cook over medium heat until soft. Add the molasses and pomegranate molasses and slowly simmer until the sauce is slightly thickened and coats the back of a cold spoon. Strain the sauce and let it cool. (This recipe yields more than you will need, but will keep for months in your refrigerator and is delicious on pork and duck).

To prepare the meatballs, in a small sauté pan over medium heat, heat the 2 tablespoons of olive oil and add the onion and garlic. Cook until the vegetables are lightly caramelized. Add the harissa, cinnamon, cumin, cayenne pepper, saffron and cilantro and cook until fragrant, about 2 minutes. Remove from the heat and let the mixture cool.

Blend the cooled seasonings into the ground chicken. Add the egg and combine well. Form into bite-sized meatballs, place them on a greased cookie sheet, and bake until the meatballs are lightly browned. Lower the oven temperature to 350°. Drizzle the browned meatballs with enough of the pomegranate sauce to coat. Cover the pan with foil and bake until the meatballs are glazed, about 20 minutes. Serve immediately, with a toothpick inserted into each meatball.

pair with huntington cellars zinfandel

Kendall-Jackson Wine Center

5007 fulton road, fulton, ca 95439
707-571-8100

www.kj.com

In the Kendall-Jackson Culinary Garden, we grow a wide variety of herbs and try to include them in our recipes whenever possible. Here is an appetizer we like to serve with our red wines; it incorporates many of the fresh herbs in the garden. Pomegranate molasses can be found in Mediterranean and Asian markets. **25 1-ounce portions**

lamb keftas

with pomegranate molasses glaze

chefs Andrei Litvinenko and Matthew Lowe

ingredients

25 8-inch bamboo skewers
1 pound ground lamb
5 ounces ground pork fat
1 teaspoon ground black pepper
½ cup yellow onion, minced fine
1 tablespoon garlic, minced fine
1 tablespoon fresh mint, minced fine
½ cup fresh parsley, minced fine
1 teaspoon fresh rosemary, minced fine
½ teaspoon cayenne pepper
½ teaspoon cumin
½ teaspoon nutmeg, fresh ground
½ teaspoon cinnamon
3 tablespoons kosher salt
¼ cup pomegranate molasses

directions soak the bamboo skewers in water for 1 hour

In a large bowl, combine all the ingredients except the skewers and pomegranate molasses. Mix thoroughly and divide into 25 portions. Take each 1-ounce portion and form it into a 3-inch-long "sausage" on each of the 25 skewers. Refrigerate the skewers until ready to grill.

In a small saucepan over low heat, heat the pomegranate molasses and slowly reduce it until it's thick and syrupy. Remove the molasses from the heat and reserve.

Grill the kefta skewers to medium-rare. Brush them with the pomegranate glaze and serve immediately.

pair with kendall-jackson highland estates merlot

La Crema Winery

3690 laughlin road, windsor, ca 95492
707-571-1504

www.lacrema.com

Asian-spiced pork meets the all-American hamburger bun and
pickles in this appetizer that can be eaten with one hand. Use
the other to hold a glass of La Crema Pinot Noir! **Serves 20**

pork belly sliders

chef Ryan Pollnow

ingredients

½ teaspoon white peppercorns
1 teaspoon coriander
½ bunch fresh cilantro
3 garlic cloves
1 fresh ginger root (about the size of your finger)
2 shallots
2 tablespoons vegetable oil
3 pounds pork belly
½ cup soy sauce
¼ cup brown sugar
1-½ cups La Crema Pinot Noir
1 quart chicken stock
1-¼ cup prepared Hoisin sauce
20 mini hamburger buns
20 sliced sandwich pickles

directions preheat oven to 275°

In a blender, grind the peppercorns, coriander, cilantro, garlic, ginger and shallots into a fine paste. Place the paste in a small frying pan and warm over low heat until just fragrant. Set aside.

In a large frying pan, heat the oil over medium heat, add the pork belly, and cook it until the outside is brown. Place the belly in a braising dish and add the soy sauce, brown sugar, wine, chicken stock and Hoisin sauce, stirring to mix and coat the meat. Bring the braising liquid to a simmer on the stove top, then cover with foil. Transfer the braising dish to the preheated oven and cook until the meat is fork-tender (about 4 hours).

Remove the pork and place it on a cookie sheet covered with plastic wrap. Wrap the pork with more plastic, place it on the cookie sheet and transfer it to the refrigerator. Place a heavy weight on top of the meat to press it down.

Meanwhile, strain the braising liquid and place it in a small saucepan. Cook on medium heat until the sauce is reduced and thick. When the refrigerated pork is cool, cut it into 2-inch strips and glaze the strips with the reduced sauce.

To serve the sliders, steam the hamburger buns until they're soft and warm. Reheat the hoisin-glazed pork belly in a large sauté pan on the stove top. Place a strip of pork belly and a pickle on each bun.

pair with la crema los carneros pinot noir

Moshin Vineyards

10295 westside road, healdsburg, ca 95448
707-433-5499

www.moshinvineyards.com

Duck has always been a classic food pairing for Pinot Noir. The Moshin family chose Tai Olesky of Mosaic Restaurant & Wine Lounge in Forestville to create an innovative recipe that would bring out the best in both duck and our Pinot Noir. Throw a Pinot Noir-themed dinner party and start your guests off with this beautiful and flavorful appetizer, which is served on risotto cakes and embellished by a rich cherry sauce. Prickly pear puree and red verjus can be found at specialty grocery stores. **Serves 12**

prickly duck

with pinot noir

chef Tai Olesky, Mosaic Restaurant & Wine Lounge

ingredients

4 duck legs
¼ cup salt
1 teaspoon sugar
1 star anise, ground
1 green cardamom, ground
¼ stick cinnamon, ground
duck fat (enough to submerge duck in chosen cooking vessel)
½ cup Pinot Noir
½ cup red verjus
1 teaspoon sugar
4 ounces dried cherries (preferably Bing)
4 ounces prickly pear puree
1 cup Arborio rice
1 tablespoon vegetable oil

directions start the duck 12 hours in advance

To prepare the duck, dust the legs generously with salt, 1 teaspoon sugar, star anise, cardamom and cinnamon. Seal tightly in a zipper-lock bag and refrigerate for 12 hours.

Remove the duck from the refrigerator, then briefly rinse and pat dry. Place the legs in a large pot or roasting pan and add enough duck fat to submerge the meat. Cover the pan tightly and cook over low heat for 10 to 12 hours, until the meat is completely tender and falling off the bone. Remove from the heat and let cool in the pan until you can comfortably remove all the skin and pull the meat off the bones.

To prepare the cherry sauce, in a small saucepan, add the Pinot Noir, verjus and 1 teaspoon of sugar and bring the mixture to a boil over medium heat. Add the cherries and the prickly pear puree. Turn off the heat and cover the pan tightly. Allow the cherries to soak for 30 minutes, until they're plump.

To prepare the risotto cakes, cook the rice as directed on the package. Once the rice is cool (you'll have approximately 2 cups), spread it on a sheet pan and press it down evenly, to about ½-inch thickness. Using a ring mold, punch out bite-sized pieces.

To serve, fry the risotto cakes in the vegetable oil until they're crispy. Place the cakes on the center of a serving plate and top each cake with a mound of duck. Spoon the cherry sauce on top of the duck and around the plate.

pair with moshin vineyards pinot noir

Paradise Ridge Winery

4545 thomas lake harris drive, santa rosa, ca 95403
707-528-9463

www.prwinery.com

This is not your mama's meat pie. These wonderfully savory appetizers match beautifully with the rich finish of our Rockpile Cabernet Sauvignon. You can also make larger portions in ramekins and serve them for dinner. **Serves 8 as an appetizer, 4 as an entrée**

torte de boeuf

with point reyes blue cheese and white truffle oil
chef Preferred Sonoma Caterers

ingredients

2 pounds boneless beef short ribs
salt and pepper
4 tablespoons vegetable oil
2 carrots, peeled and diced
1 small onion, diced
2 tablespoons tomato paste
2 bay leaves
½ teaspoon dried thyme
2 cups Paradise Ridge Rockpile Cabernet Sauvignon
2 cups beef stock
1 tablespoons butter
2 tablespoons flour
4 tablespoons white truffle oil
your favorite pie crust dough (unbaked)
¼ cup Point Reyes Blue Cheese, crumbled

directions preheat oven to 350°

Season the short ribs with salt and pepper. In a deep roasting pan, heat 4 tablespoons of oil over medium heat and brown the ribs. Remove the meat to a plate, add the carrots and onion to the pan, and sauté until golden. Add the tomato paste, bay leaves and thyme and stir to blend the ingredients.

Return the ribs to the pan and cover them with the Cabernet Sauvignon and beef stock. Bake for 3 to 4 hours, until the meat is fork-tender. Remove the bay leaves and drain and reserve the liquid; allow the liquid and ribs to cool.

In a saucepan over medium heat, make a roux by melting the butter and stirring in the flour. Slowly stir in the cooking liquid until the mixture thickens.

With two forks, shred the beef and add it to the thickened sauce. Add the truffle oil and allow to cool completely.

Line miniature muffin cups with the pie dough. Place 1 to 2 tablespoons of beef filling in each cup and top with a crumble of blue cheese. Bake for 22 to 25 minutes, or until golden.

pair with with paradise ridge rockpile cabernet sauvignon

Sapphire Hill Winery

51 front street, healdsburg, ca 95448
707-431-1888

www.sapphirehill.com

"When I want to impress my dinner guests, I like to make something special, something they might not normally have on a regular basis, and this foie gras appetizer really does the job," says Sapphire Hill owner Anne Giere. "While fairly simple to prepare, make sure to allow enough lead time for all the marinating and refrigeration involved. This torchon is so decadent, you just might feel guilty eating even a little bit. But don't feel too sinful … some of life's finer things are its forbidden pleasures." **Serves 10**

foie gras torchon

chef Job Carder, Executive Chef, Manzanita Restaurant

ingredients

1-½ pounds foie gras
2 cups Madeira wine
1-½ ounces salt
4 pinches white pepper, ground
1 pinch clove, ground
1 pinch cinnamon, ground
1 pinch nutmeg, ground
1 pinch black pepper, ground
6 cups chicken stock
2 cups apple cider
2 cups apple cider vinegar
French bread slices, grilled

directions start this dish 24 hours in advance

Devein the foie gras and pass it through a fine-mesh sieve. Re-mold the foie gras together in one piece and spread it flat and evenly over an 8x18 sheet pan lined with parchment paper.

In a saucepan over medium heat, reduce the Madeira until it reaches a syrupy consistency, then let it cool. Sprinkle the salt and all the spices evenly over the foie gras, then brush it evenly with the reduced Madeira. Place the foie gras in a plastic resealable bag and let it marinate in the refrigerator for 24 hours.

The next day, cut the foie gras into three same-size squares, including the parchment paper, and let the squares sit at room temperature until they soften. When the pieces are soft, use the parchment paper to roll the foie gras squares into tight, rounded logs or cylinders, removing the paper as you go. Then wrap each of the cylinders tightly in cheesecloth and tie both ends with string.

In a large saucepan, bring the chicken stock to a boil over medium-high heat, then turn down to a simmer. Poach each foie gras log in the stock for 30 seconds, then remove and let them cool in the refrigerator.

Once cool, remove the used cheesecloth and discard it. Re-roll the foie gras in a double layer of fresh cheesecloth, with approximately 2 inches of extra length of cloth on each side. Tie the logs at both ends with string. Tie additional lengths of string, spaced 1 inch apart, around the girth of the cylinder, wrapping each foie gras log tightly. Refrigerate for several hours.

In a medium saucepan, mix together the apple cider and apple cider vinegar and cook over medium heat, reducing the liquid until it's syrupy. Let cool.

Each torchon yields 10 slices. Serve 3 slices per person on lightly grilled bread, add a sprinkle of French sea salt and a drop or two of the apple syrup.

pair with sapphire hill russian river valley pinot noir

Stephen & Walker Winery

243 healdsburg avenue, healdsburg, ca 95448
707-431-8749

www.trustwine.com

My two sons, Walker and Duncan, love these treats so much that they've declared the recipe to be a new family tradition, and even volunteer to help prepare it. **Serves 10 to 12**

grilled bruschetta

with rosemary-white bean puree and heirloom tomatoes

chef Nancy Walker

ingredients

¾ cup extra-virgin olive oil; more as needed
4 cloves garlic, smashed and peeled
two 3-inch sprigs plus 1 teaspoon fresh rosemary, chopped
2 large heirloom tomatoes, cut into half-inch cubes
1-½ teaspoons kosher salt
1 15-ounce can cannellini beans, rinsed well and drained
⅓ cup freshly grated Parmigiano-Reggiano cheese
1 to 2 tablespoons fresh lemon juice
½ teaspoon ground black pepper
1 large baguette, cut into ½-inch slices

directions

In a small saucepan, heat the oil, garlic and rosemary sprigs over medium heat, until they start to sizzle steadily and become fragrant, about 2 to 3 minutes. Let the oil cool to room temperature, then strain it into a measuring cup.

Place the tomatoes in a medium bowl and toss with 3 tablespoons of the garlic olive oil and 1 teaspoon of salt.

Put the beans in a food processor and add 6 tablespoons of the garlic oil, the grated cheese, 1 tablespoon of lemon juice, the remaining 1 teaspoon of chopped rosemary, the remaining ½ teaspoon of salt and the black pepper. Puree until just smooth. Season to taste with salt, pepper and lemon juice.

To prepare the bruschettas, heat a gas grill to medium-high, or prepare a medium-hot charcoal fire. Brush both sides of the baguette slices with the remaining garlic oil (if you run out, use plain olive oil). Sprinkle the bread slices lightly with salt and grill them until they're crisp and with grill marks on both sides, 1 to 2 minutes per side.

Spread the bean puree on the bread slices, top with a generous spoonful of the tomatoes and their juices, and sprinkle lightly with pepper. Serve on a large platter and watch them disappear.

pair with stephen & walker dry creek valley sauvignon blanc

Taft Street Winery

2030 barlow lane, sebastopol, ca 95472
707-823-2049

www.taftstreetwinery.com

Taft Street president Mike Tierney has been serving this dish at winery parties for several years. The recipe originated in our garden, where we grow as many as 30 kinds of tomatoes. A few years ago, we went overboard and planted six San Marzano vines; each vine yields up to 100 tomatoes, so we had to think of ways to make best use of this bounty. After sun-drying the tomatoes and trying various methods of slow roasting, we found this method to be perhaps the tastiest, as the basil and bacon are natural partners for tomatoes. The tomatoes can be preserved by packing them in olive oil. **Serves 24**

blt, taft street style

ingredients

12 plum tomatoes (preferably San Marzano)
3 tablespoons olive oil
1 shallot, chopped
¼ cup fresh basil, chopped
salt
pepper
24 medium basil leaves
6 slices cooked bacon (good quality), quartered
Parmigiano-Reggiano cheese, grated

directions preheat oven to 275°

Slice the tomatoes in half lengthwise, and remove the seeds and liquid. Place the tomatoes on a baking sheet that has been rubbed with 1 tablespoon of the oil. Sprinkle the shallot and chopped basil over the tomatoes, season with salt and pepper, and drizzle the remaining 2 tablespoons of oil over the tomatoes. Roast the tomatoes for 2-½ to 3 hours, or until they are chewy yet still flexible.

Place the cooked tomatoes on a large serving plate. Put a basil leaf on each tomato, then top with a piece of bacon. Sprinkle grated cheese over the top.

pair with taft street sonoma coast pinot noir

Trentadue Winery

19170 geyserville avenue, geyserville, ca 95441
707-433-3104

www.trentadue.com

Despite the savory ingredients in this recipe, the mousse is actually nicely sweet. The port and Zinfandel in the sauce adds the sweetness, and the creamy fresh goat cheese (chevre) and orange zest give this dish a bright, clean flavor. Serve the mousse on toasted crostini. **Serves 4 to 8**

appetizers

leo's zin-fulicious

citrus-chevre mousse

chef Allison Creager

ingredients

Sauce

2 cups Trentadue Sonoma County Zinfandel
½ cup Trentadue Zinfandel Port
1 teaspoon whole black peppercorns
2 sprigs fresh thyme
1 shallot, minced
1 cup sugar

Goat Cheese Mousse

12 ounces fresh goat cheese
4 tablespoons whipping cream
1 teaspoon fresh thyme, chopped
1 tablespoon orange zest, grated

Crostini

1 French baguette, sliced and toasted
½ cup walnuts, toasted and chopped

directions

To prepare the sauce, combine all the ingredients in a medium saucepan and cook over medium heat, until the mixture is reduced to the consistency of syrup. Let cool.

To prepare the mousse, in a medium bowl, combine all the ingredients and blend until smooth and creamy.

To serve, toast the baguette slices and spread with the mousse. Drizzle the sauce on top of the mousse and sprinkle with the walnuts.

pair with trentadue sonoma county zinfandel

soups

Amphora Winery

4791 dry creek road, building 6, healdsburg, ca 95448
707-431-7767

www.amphorawines.com

This is the perfect recipe for using the last-of-the-season tomatoes from the garden in early autumn. Don't attempt this recipe unless you have vine-ripened tomatoes. Roasting gives the tomatoes a rich, savory flavor that pairs beautifully with our ripe, juicy Dry Creek Valley Syrah. **Serves 6 to 8**

a midsummer night's
cream of tomato soup

chef Jim Walter

ingredients

2 pounds ripe plum tomatoes (preferably San Marzano)
8 tablespoons olive oil
1 teaspoon black pepper, freshly ground
1 teaspoon dried basil
½ teaspoon dried Greek oregano
¾ cup onion, finely minced
4 cloves garlic, finely minced
1 cup chicken or vegetable stock
¾ cup heavy cream
½ teaspoon balsamic vinegar

directions preheat oven to 475°

Cut the tomatoes in half lengthwise, and gently mix them in a large bowl with half of the olive oil and all of the pepper, basil and oregano, until the tomatoes are evenly coated. Spread the tomatoes, cut side down, in a non-reactive baking pan, and roast in the oven until the edges of the tomatoes are very dark, about 25 to 35 minutes. Remove the pan from the oven and allow the tomatoes to cool for several minutes.

Place the cooled tomatoes in a food processor, along with the oil/herb mixture scraped from the baking pan, and process until not quite smooth.

In a large saucepan over medium heat, combine the onion, garlic and remaining 4 tablespoons of oil. Cook until the garlic is a light-golden color and the onions are translucent, lowering the heat if necessary to avoid scorching. Add the tomato mixture to the saucepan, whisk in the stock, and bring the mixture to a simmer. Cook for about 10 minutes, then lower the heat and whisk in the cream and balsamic vinegar.

Season with salt and pepper to taste, and serve the soup in bowls with crusty country bread on the side.

pair with amphora syrah

Everett Ridge Vineyards & Winery

435 west dry creek road, healdsburg, ca 95448
707-433-1637

www.everettridge.com

Chris Sterling, our "chief chef at all events," wanted to make a soup that is similar to the one his wife Andrea's mother made. His mother-in-law's recipe calls for pigeon peas, legumes that are common in the Caribbean yet not easy to find here, so he substituted lentils for the pigeon peas. The only problem is, Chris is allergic to lentils and can't eat his own soup. The good news is that there is more for the rest of us. **Serves 4 to 6**

zinful harvest soup

chef Chris Sterling

ingredients

2 tablespoons olive oil
1 medium onion, chopped
2 celery stalks, diced
1 carrot, diced
½ pound chicken apple sausage, sliced
2 garlic cloves, minced
1 30-ounce can crushed tomatoes
5 cups chicken broth
½ cup lentils
½ cup Everett Ridge Zinfandel
salt and pepper to taste

directions

Place the oil, onion, celery, carrot and sausage in a large saucepan. Cook over medium heat for about 10 minutes, until the vegetables are wilted, then add the garlic and cook for 2 to 3 more minutes.

Add the tomatoes, broth and lentils and bring to a boil. Reduce the heat and simmer for 20 minutes. Add the Zinfandel and season the soup with salt and pepper. Cook for an additional 20 minutes, then serve.

pair with everett ridge zinfandel

Family Wineries, Dry Creek Valley

4791 dry creek road, healdsburg, ca 95448
707-433-0100

www.familywines.com

There is Gumby, and there is Dumbo, and then there is gumbo—a melting pot of New Orleans flavors that brings out the spice in both people and wine. Our recipe will be enjoyed by those who like a little peppery snap in their lives, and who are more jammy and over-the-top. Join our melting pot of Dry Creek Valley wineries in matching with this eclectic wine and food pairing. **Serves 8**

gumbo

with chicken and andouille sausage

chef Jeff Mall, Chef/Owner, Zin Restaurant & Wine Bar

ingredients

Dark Roux

3 tablespoons flour
3 tablespoons vegetable oil

Steamed Rice

1-¾ cups water
1 cup long-grain white rice
1 teaspoon salt

Gumbo

1 tablespoon olive oil
1 link andouille sausage, diced
8 chicken thighs, seasoned with salt and pepper
2 medium yellow onions, diced
1 cup celery, diced
2 green bell peppers, seeded and diced
4 cloves garlic, smashed
1 cup dry sherry wine
1 tablespoon Worchestershire sauce
½ teaspoon red pepper flakes
2 bay leaves
1 teaspoon fresh thyme, minced
1 tablespoon tomato paste
4 cups chicken stock
kosher salt
black pepper
Tabasco sauce (optional)

directions start the roux 1 hour ahead; have steamed rice ready when the gumbo is done

To prepare the roux, combine the flour and oil together in a small pot and cook over low heat until the mixture turns a deep mahogany color, stirring often. This can take up to 1 hour. Let cool.

To prepare the gumbo, heat the 1 tablespoon of olive oil in a large pot and sauté the sausage until it's well-browned. Add the seasoned chicken thighs, skin side down. Cook for 5 minutes. Turn the thighs over and add the onions, celery, green peppers and garlic. Cook for 10 minutes over medium heat, or until the vegetables are translucent.

Add the sherry, Worchestershire sauce, red pepper flakes, bay leaves, thyme and tomato paste. Add the chicken stock and bring to a boil. Reduce to a simmer and stir in the roux. Season with salt and pepper, and cook for 45 minutes.

To prepare the rice, in a medium saucepan, bring the water to a boil, stir in the rice, cover the pan and reduce the heat to low. Cook for 15 minutes. Remove the rice from the heat and let it sit for 5 minutes.

Serve the gumbo in large bowls, ladeling it over the rice. Add Tabasco sauce if you like it spicy.

pair with philip staley grenache, lago di merlo ca'bella vino rosso, mietz syrah, dashe cellars louvau zinfandel, collier falls primitivo and forth rosé of syrah

Geyser Peak Winery

22281 chianti road, geyserville, ca 95441
707-857-9400

www.geyserpeakwinery.com

One of our favorite caterers, Dan Lucia, enjoys warming the souls of visitors to our winery. This year we asked him to develop a hearty soup that can be savored with both red and white wine. His corn chowder creation is perfect for a brisk fall evening in front of a roaring fire. Enjoy! **Serves 8**

corn chowder

with apple-smoked bacon

chef Dan Lucia

ingredients

1 pound apple-smoked bacon, sliced into narrow strips
4 tablespoons olive oil
1 large fennel bulb, chopped
1 large yellow onion, chopped
1 large red onion, chopped
4 garlic cloves, minced
4 celery stalks, diced
2 medium leeks, sliced (white and light green parts only)

1 cup heavy cream
10 cups chicken or vegetable stock
4 cups yellow corn, cut from the cob
4 cups white corn, cut from the cob
2 tablespoons cumin
3 tablespoons fresh thyme, stems removed
2 russet potatoes, peeled and diced
salt and white pepper to taste

directions

In a large stock pot, sauté the bacon and set it aside. In the same pan, add the olive oil, fennel, onions and garlic and sauté until the vegetables are soft. Add the celery and leeks and continue to sauté for 5 more minutes.

Add the heavy cream and stock, and bring to a simmer. Add the corn and continue to cook for 20 minutes. Add the cumin, thyme, potatoes and pre-cooked bacon, and continue cooking for 30 more minutes, or until the potatoes are tender. Season to taste with salt and white pepper.

pair with geyser peak white or red wine

Kendall-Jackson, Healdsburg

337 healdsburg avenue, healdsburg, ca 95448
707-433-7102

www.kj.com

This classic dish is served in Mexican and Spanish homes and combines albondigas (meatballs) with a spicy soup packed with garden vegetables. We love this soup on an autumn night with a luscious red wine, such as our Highland Estates Trace Ridge Cabernet Sauvignon. **Serves 6**

albondigas

in spicy chipotle broth

chefs Matthew Lowe and Alfredo Reyes

ingredients

Meatballs

¾ pound ground beef
½ pound ground pork
¼ cup bread crumbs
¼ cup minced onion
½ teaspoon cumin
¼ teaspoon chipotle powder
1 large egg, beaten
salt and pepper to taste

Soup

1 tablespoon olive oil
1 large garlic clove, minced
½ cup yellow onion, diced
1 carrot, diced
3 stalks celery, diced
½ teaspoon ground cumin
1 teaspoon oregano (preferably Mexican)
6 cups chicken broth
1 16-ounce can diced tomatoes
1 chipotle chile in adobo sauce (1 chile, not the whole can)
1 zucchini, sliced
¼ cup uncooked white rice
cilantro for garnish, chopped

directions

Make the meatballs first. In a large bowl, combine all the ingredients and mix thoroughly. Using your hands, form the mixture into approximately 25 bite-sized meatballs and set aside.

To prepare the soup, heat the oil in a heavy pot over medium heat. Sauté the garlic, onion, carrot and celery until the onion is soft. Then add the cumin and oregano, and heat for about 1 minute to open the flavors. Add the chicken broth, tomatoes and chile, stir, and bring to a slight boil. Gently drop in the meatballs, one at a time, reduce the heat, and simmer for 10 minutes.

Add the zucchini and rice. Cover and simmer for 20 minutes, or until the rice is tender. Season with salt and pepper, and garnish with the cilantro.

pair with kendall-jackson highland estates trace ridge cabernet sauvignon

Lake Sonoma Winery

340 healdsburg avenue, healdsburg, ca 95448
707-473-2999

www.lakesonomawinery.com

Although this soup may sound a little strange, don't judge it until
you taste it! This smooth, creamy chowder is an autumn favorite
in Sonoma County, where crisp, juicy Gravenstein apples grow.
Served with a loaf of artisan bread and sweet butter, there is
nothing better to eat on a cool, misty evening. If you can't find
Gravenstein apples, use Fuji or Gala instead. **Serves 6**

potato soup

with gravenstein apples and cheddar cheese

chef Robin Lehnhoff McCray

ingredients

2 tablespoons olive oil
3 Gravenstein apples, peeled, cored and diced
2 russet potatoes, peeled and diced
½ cup celery, chopped
½ cup yellow onion, chopped
1 teaspoon kosher salt
½ cup Lake Sonoma Chardonnay
6 cups chicken or vegetable stock
1 teaspoon fresh thyme leaves
2 cups sharp white cheddar cheese, grated
½ cup heavy cream
1 pinch nutmeg
¼ teaspoon white pepper

directions

In a large pot, heat the oil and sauté the apples, potatoes, celery and onion until soft. Season with the salt. Add the wine and simmer for 5 minutes. Add the stock and simmer for 30 minutes more.

Remove the soup from the heat and puree it in a blender until smooth, working in batches if necessary. Return the mixture to the pot and add the thyme, cheese, cream, nutmeg and white pepper. Heat just until the soup is hot—don't let it boil because the cheese will curdle—and serve.

pair with lake sonoma chardonnay

Simi Winery

16275 healdsburg avenue, healdsburg, ca 95448
707-433-6981

www.simiwinery.com

(For this savory seafood stew, prepare the rouille, a piquant sauce
that is added to the soup just before serving, in advance. Store
it in the refrigerator until you're ready to start the soup. **Serves 8**)

bouillabaisse à la simi

with rouille

chef Eric Lee

ingredients

Rouille

1 ounce red wine vinegar
1 tablespoon lemon juice
1 egg yolk
1 small potato, boiled and peeled
4 cloves garlic
1 tablespoon tomato paste
1/8 teaspoon cayenne pepper
1/4 teaspoon paprika
pinch salt and pepper
12 ounces olive oil

Bouillabaisse

1 ounce olive oil
1 onion, chopped
2 ribs celery, chopped
4 cloves garlic, chopped
1 fennel bulb, chopped
6 Roma tomatoes, chopped
2 sprigs thyme
1 bay leaf
1 teaspoon orange zest
large pinch saffron
1 ounce brandy
1 cup Simi Chardonnay
24 ounces seafood stock or low-sodium chicken stock
1 pound firm white fish
2 pounds assorted raw seafood
  (shrimp, scallops, mussels, squid)
2 tablespoons Italian flat parsley, chopped
2 tablespoons basil, sliced into thin strips

directions

To prepare the rouille, place all the ingredients except the olive oil in a food processor. Process for 4 seconds, and with the blade still running, slowly add the oil in a thin stream to emulsify, forming a thick mayonnaise. Add more salt and pepper to taste, and store in the refrigerator until ready to serve.

To prepare the bouillabaisse, heat the oil in a heavy-bottomed saucepan and sauté the onion, celery, garlic, fennel and tomatoes until soft, about 8 minutes. Add the thyme, bay leaf, orange zest and saffron and cook for 2 minutes more. Remove the pan from the heat, add the brandy, and quickly return the pan to the heat. Tipping the pan away your body, ignite the brandy fumes at the edge of the pan (but not the liquid itself) with a long match or barbecue lighter. When the flames disappear, add the Chardonnay and cook to reduce the liquid by half.

Add the stock and bring to a simmer. Add the white fish and cook until just done. Remove the fish and set aside. Similarly, add the raw seafood, one variety at a time, and cook it until just done, then remove and repeat with the next type of seafood. Strain the liquid through a strainer, pressing hard to get all of the liquid. To serve, reheat the liquid and check the seasoning. Divide the fish and seafood equally among 8 warmed bowls and add the warmed liquid. Top with a big dollop of the rouille and the chopped parsley and basil.

pair with simi alexander valley chardonnay

Toad Hollow Vineyards

409-A healdsburg avenue, healdsburg, ca 95448
707-431-8667

www.toadhollow.com

This hearty soup has an abundance of ingredients yet is easy to make. It can be made vegetarian by omitting the pancetta and using vegetable stock instead of chicken or beef stock. Optional ingredients such as fresh vegetables (peas, cubed zucchini and crookneck squash, and chopped spinach and chard), cannellini beans and small dried pasta will give the soup more dimension of flavor and texture. There are no exact measurements for the optional ingredients, as that's the way Debbie's father taught her to prepare this dish, adding a little of this and a little of that. It takes some time for the flavors to meld, so pour a glass of Toad Hollow Cacophony Zinfandel and enjoy the process. **Serves 6 to 8**

minestrone soup

chef Debbie Rickards

ingredients

Minestrone

1 tablespoon extra virgin olive oil
2 tablespoons butter
4 to 6 ounces pancetta, chopped
1 large onion, chopped
4 to 6 garlic cloves, minced
1 pinch red pepper flakes (optional)
1 32-ounce can chicken, beef or vegetable stock
2 bay leaves
½ teaspoon dried parsley
½ teaspoon dried sage
½ teaspoon dried oregano
½ teaspoon dried thyme
½ teaspoon dried basil
2 stalks celery, sliced into quarter moons
2 carrots, sliced into rounds
2 large potatoes, peeled and left whole
2 tablespoons tomato paste
1 28-ounce can San Marzano tomatoes
Several Parmesan cheese rinds, trimmed and saved from large wedges
salt and black pepper to taste

Pesto Topping

1 large bunch basil, washed, dried and chopped
½ cup extra virgin olive oil
2 to 4 garlic cloves
2 to 4 tablespoons toasted pine nuts
¼ cup Parmesan cheese, grated
¼ cup Romano cheese, grated
salt to taste

directions

To prepare the soup, combine the olive oil and butter in a large stock pot. Add the pancetta and onion and sauté for 8 to 10 minutes, or until soft. Add the garlic and red pepper flakes and sauté for 1 or 2 minutes longer—don't let the garlic burn. Add the stock and the rest of the ingredients. Bring to a gentle boil, then immediately reduce to a simmer and continue cooking for about 2 hours. The rinds of the cheese will soften and add a wonderful flavor to the soup. Leave the potatoes whole so they do not completely fall apart; you can break them up before serving.

To prepare the pesto, combine all the ingredients in a food processor, reserving half of the olive oil and adding it as needed to get the pesto to a smooth consistency. Remove to a small bowl for serving at the table. The pesto can be made in advance, but be sure to cover it with plastic wrap and press the plastic directly onto the surface of the pesto, to prevent it from turning brown. Refrigerate until ready to use.

To serve, ladle the minestrone into bowls and invite diners to add a dollop of pesto.

pair with toad hollow cacophony zinfandel

Wilson Winery

1960 dry creek road, healdsburg, ca 95448
707-433-4355

www.wilsonwinery.com

"A Wine & Food Affair" wouldn't be complete without our famous marinated tri-tip. This year we serve it with a rich potato-leek soup. Marinate the tri-tip overnight and prepare the croutons before starting the soup. **Serves 8 (both recipes)**

potato leek soup

with truffle crouton paired with Wilson Winery's famous marinated tri-tip

chef Mike Matson, Vintage Valley Catering (soup) and chef Tom (tri-tip)

ingredients

Tri-tip
2 cups soy sauce
½ cup Wilson Winery Cabernet Sauvignon
3 cloves garlic, minced
2 teaspoons fresh-ground black pepper
1 tri-tip, about 3 pounds

Soup
4 leeks, sliced
2 Maui or yellow onions, diced
3 teaspoons fresh thyme, chopped
10 russet potatoes, peeled and cubed
6 cups vegetable broth
1-½ cups heavy cream

Croutons
½ baguette, cut into ½-inch cubes
black truffle oil
olive oil

directions

To prepare the tri-tip, combine the soy sauce, wine, garlic and black pepper in a bowl. Place the tri-tip in a container and pour the marinade over the meat. Cover and refrigerate overnight.

Prepare a fire in a grill. Remove the tri-tip from the marinade and grill until medium-rare. Transfer to a cutting board and slice the meat thinly across the grain.

To prepare the croutons, preheat the oven to 350°. Arrange the baguette cubes on a baking pan, drizzle with truffle oil and olive oil, and bake until they're crisp, about 10 minutes.

To prepare the soup, in a medium stock pot, wilt the leeks, onions and thyme. Add the diced potatoes and vegetable broth. Simmer until the potatoes are tender, add the heavy cream, and mash or blend together well. Garnish with the croutons.

pair with wilson cabernet sauvignon

Windsor Oaks Vineyards

10810 hillview road, windsor, ca 95492
707-433-4050

www.windsoroaks.com

This is an incredibly easy dish to prepare, yet it tastes far more luxurious than its simplicity would indicate. The "decadence" comes from the black truffle oil, which can be found in gourmet markets and some large grocery stores. **Serves 6 to 8**

decadent bisque

with mushrooms and truffle oil

chef Julie Hagler Lumgair

ingredients

1 stick (4 ounces) butter
2 teaspoons dried thyme
1 yellow onion, chopped
8 ounces crimini mushrooms, sliced
16 tablespoons flour
5 cups vegetable, mushroom or chicken stock
2 cups heavy cream
¼ cup black truffle oil

directions

Melt the butter in a large stock pot. Add the thyme, onion and mushrooms, and sauté until the onions are soft. Add the flour 1 tablespoon at a time, stirring constantly, and cook for 2 to 3 minutes. Add the stock and whisk thoroughly. When the bisque begins to thicken, gently whisk in the heavy cream.

To serve, ladle the bisque into bowls and drizzle the surface of each with the black truffle oil.

pair with windsor oaks estate pinot noir, zinfandel, cabernet sauvignon or chardonnay

salads & sides

Johnson's Alexander Valley Wines

8333 highway 128, healdsburg, ca 95448
707-433-2319

www.johnsonavwines.com

This is a great salad for summer and it pairs beautifully with crisp white wines. Mom (Gail) always said it was the only salad for which men came back for seconds. This recipe is easy to make, and we cannot have a lunch or dinner event at the winery without serving it. Mom always added pine nuts to this salad, but I don't like nuts, so I leave them out. Feel free to add them to the recipe. **Serves 10**

gail's feta salad

with poppy seed dressing
chef Ellen Johnson

ingredients

Poppy Seed Dressing
1-½ cups granulated sugar
2 teaspoons dry mustard
2 teaspoons salt
3 tablespoons juice from 1 yellow onion
²/₃ cup white vinegar
2 cups salad oil
1 tablespoon poppy seeds

Salad
1 large bag mixed salad greens
1 small bag fancy lettuces, such as spring mix
2 baskets red cherry tomatoes, halved
1 red onion, thinly sliced
1 cup feta cheese, crumbled
raw pine nuts, to taste

directions

To prepare the dressing, combine the sugar, mustard, salt, onion juice and vinegar in a food processor or blender. Mix well, then slowly add the oil while continuing to blend. Add the poppy seeds. Refrigerate the dressing for at least 1 hour before serving (you will have approximately 1 quart).

To prepare the salad, in a large salad bowl, combine the two bags of greens, tomatoes, onion and feta and toss with approximately half the dressing, adding dressing gradually until the lettuces are lightly coated. Refrigerate the remaining dressing, where it will keep for about 5 days.

pair with johnson's alexander valley chardonnay

La Crema Tasting Room

235 healdsburg avenue, healdsburg, ca 95448
707-431-9400

www.lacrema.com

The original recipe for this dish calls for chicken confit, which requires the slow-cooking of a dozen chicken legs and thighs with a coating of duck fat. Yet surprisingly little flavor is lost when home-roasted or store-bought rotisserie chicken is substituted for confit. If you can't find fresh cranberries, use frozen. **Serves 20**

wild rice pudding

with savory bread, roasted squash and chicken

chef Taki Laliotitis

ingredients

2 tablespoons butter
2 shallots, minced
½ cup fresh or frozen cranberries (thawed)
¼ cup dried cherries
9 cups chicken stock
2 cups wild rice, uncooked
1 tablespoon kosher salt
1 tablespoon fresh thyme, minced
1 cup butternut squash, peeled and cut into ¼-inch dice
1 cup shredded chicken meat
2 cups heavy cream
10 large eggs
8 cups white bread, diced and air-dried

kosher salt, to taste
black pepper, to taste

directions preheat oven to 350°

Heat an 8-quart pot over medium heat and add 1 tablespoon of the butter. Once the butter is melted, add the shallots and cook until they're wilted, about 1 minute. Add the cranberries and cook for 1 minute.

Add the dried cherries, chicken stock, wild rice and 1 tablespoon of salt. Bring to a boil and reduce to a simmer. Cover and simmer for 45 minutes, until the rice puffs open. Strain any remaining liquid from the rice and set the rice aside. Over medium heat, reduce the excess liquid to 1 cup, then mix the rice back in.

Place an oven-proof pan into the 350° oven for 10 minutes, then add to it the remaining 1 tablespoon of butter, thyme and squash. Season with salt and pepper, then roast until golden brown and tender, about 15 minutes. Remove the squash mixture from the oven and let it cool.

In a large bowl, combine the cooked rice, squash, chicken, cream, eggs and bread. Adjust the seasonings. Bake the "pudding" in a large casserole dish until golden brown, and serve warm.

pair with la crema anderson valley pinot noir

Matrix Winery

3291 westside road, healdsburg, ca 95448
707-433-1911

www.matrixwinery.com

We have our neighbors at Costeaux Bakery in Healdsburg
to thank for this recipe, which makes a wonderful sandwich
of salmon, bacon, fresh tomatoes and baby greens. You
can stuff the focaccia with just about anything, or top it with
sun-dried tomatoes, goat cheese or olives. **Serves 8 to 10**

salads & sides

costeaux bakery

Focaccia

ingredients

2 cups bread flour
¼ teaspoon salt
2 teaspoons olive oil
¾ cup whole milk
1-¼-ounce package fresh active yeast, crumbled
olive oil for brushing the focaccia
salt for seasoning

directions preheat oven to 400°

Combine the first 5 ingredients in a large bowl. Mix by hand or with an electric mixer fitted with a dough hook, for 8 to 12 minutes, until the mixture is well-combined. Finish by hand, kneading the dough until it's smooth. Remove the dough to a clean bowl and cover it with plastic wrap or a clean cloth, then place it in a warm spot (preferably 75° or higher). Let the dough double in size.

Remove the dough from the bowl and divide it in half. Place each piece on a sheet pan or pizza stone and flatten and dimple the dough with your hands and fingers to make approximately 2 10-inch rounds. Brush each round with olive oil and top with a sprinkling of salt. Bake at 400° until done, approximately 30 to 40 minutes.

pair with matrix red bordeaux blend

Raymond Burr Vineyards

8339 west dry creek road, healdsburg, ca 95448
707-433-8559

www.raymondburrvineyards.com

I am originally from the Azores, west of Portugal, and this recipe for "beans of my Azorean grandmother" is from my own grandmother, Ana Costa, who used to make this dish for family gatherings, serving it as a side dish for meat or chicken. The next day, we would reheat the leftovers and serve the beans with a fried egg on top. Linguica, a spicy Portuguese pork sausage, can be found in most supermarkets. **Serves 8 to 10**

feijao da avo acoreana

"beans of my Azorean grandmother"

chef Francisco Baptista

ingredients

1 32-ounce bag dried pinto beans
10 ounces salt pork
1 tablespoon vegetable oil
1 pound linguica, cut into ¼-inch slices
2 medium yellow onions, sliced
2 bay leaves
¼ cup brown sugar
1 cinnamon stick
1 tablespoon paprika
1-½ tablespoons allspice, ground
1 clove garlic, minced
1 18-ounce can stewed tomatoes

salt to taste
bottled hot sauce to taste

directions

Cover the beans with water and soak them overnight, changing the water twice.

Add the salt pork to the beans and the final soaking water, and cook over medium heat for 20 to 30 minutes, until the meat is half-done. While the beans continue to cook for 45 minutes to 1 hour longer, remove the pork and cut it into half-inch cubes. Place the cubes in a large sauté pan with the vegetable oil, linguica and onions, and cook over medium heat until the onions are browned.

When the beans are just tender, remove them from the heat, and pour off and reserve the water.

Add the cooked meat and onions to the beans. Blend the remaining ingredients together and add to the bean mixture. Transfer the mixture to an oiled casserole dish and bake at 350° until cooked through, about 45 minutes to 1 hour. If the dish appears dry at any time during baking, add some of the reserved water.

To serve, remove the cinnamon stick and add salt and hot sauce to taste.

pair with raymond burr cabernet sauvignon and cabernet franc

Rodney Strong Vineyards

11455 old redwood highway, healdsburg, ca 95448
707-431-1533

www.rodneystrong.com

(Panko is the term for Japanese bread crumbs, which typically are lighter and crispier than traditional bread crumbs. They add a crunchy coating to these croquettes, which are delicious when dipped into homemade or store-bought marinara sauce. Look for panko at Asian specialty stores and some large supermarkets; if you can't find it, substitute with the unflavored bread crumbs of your choice. **Serves 10**)

risotto-butternut squash

croquettes

chefs Todd Muir and John Littlewood, Wine Country Chefs

ingredients

3 tablespoon butter, plus 2 tablespoons
2 cups Arborio rice
1 cup white wine
6 to 8 cups hot chicken or vegetable stock
2½ cups butternut squash, peeled and cut into very small cubes
¼ cup grated fresh Parmesan cheese
1 package panko or plain French bread crumbs
3 cups canola oil, for frying
marinara sauce (optional)

directions

In a large heavy pot, melt 3 tablespoons of butter over medium heat. Add the rice. Heat and stir to coat the rice evenly with the butter. Add the white wine and cook until the wine has almost evaporated.

Add 2 cups of stock and stir until it's absorbed, about 5 to 6 minutes. Add the squash cubes and continue cooking and adding stock, 1 cup at a time, stirring, until the rice is creamy and tender, yet still firm in the middle. Cooking should take about 20 to 25 minutes from the time you first add the stock. Remove from the heat and stir in the remaining butter and cheese, then allow to cool for 5 to 10 minutes.

Place the risotto in a pastry bag with a ¾-inch plain round tip (or a plastic bag with the corner cut off to make a ¾-inch hole). Spread the bread crumbs onto a baking sheet and "pipe" the risotto onto the crumbs in "ropes" the length of the pan. Cut the ropes into 2-inch portions, and roll them in the bread crumbs to coat them evenly.

Heat the oil to 350° in a frying pan with high sides (to prevent splattering). Fry 4 or 5 croquettes at a time for 1 to 2 minutes, or until browned all over. Serve them warm with marinara sauce on the side.

pair with rodney strong estate russian river valley pinot noir

Thumbprint Cellars

36 north street, healdsburg, ca 95448
707-433-2393

www.thumbprintcellars.com

Focaccia con verdure arrostite ("bread with roasted vegetables")
sandwiches are the perfect pairing with many Thumbprint
wines, but we especially love the way the pesto plays with
the fruitiness of our Syrah and how the herbs in the focaccia
bread dance with the earthiness of Cabernet Sauvignon.
Adding the grilled seasonal vegetables and using store-bought
pesto sauce makes this an easy-to-prepare yet complex
dish that can be served at any temperature, year-round. What
more can you ask from a food and wine pairing? **Serves 8**

focaccia

con verdure arrostite — "with roasted vegetables"
chef Luca Citti, Owner, Café Citti

ingredients

Roasted Vegetables
¼ cup balsamic vinegar
1 cup extra virgin olive oil
1 pinch fresh thyme
1 teaspoon dried oregano
juice from ½ Meyer lemon
1 clove garlic, smashed
salt and pepper to taste
2 bunches asparagus, stalks cut in half lengthwise
1 green bell pepper, seeded and cut into 1-inch-wide strips
1 red bell pepper, seeded and cut into 1-inch-wide strips
1 yellow bell pepper, seeded and cut into 1-inch-wide strips
2 medium leeks, trimmed (white & pale-green parts only) & quartered
5 zucchini squash, cut in half-inch-thick strips
5 yellow squash, cut in half-inch-thick strips

Focaccia
1 ounce fresh yeast (preferred) or 2 packages dry yeast
1 teaspoon sugar
1-¾ cups lukewarm water (105 to115°)
¹/₃ cup extra virgin olive oil, plus extra to drizzle on bread
1-½ teaspoons table salt
4 to 5-½ cups unbleached all-purpose flour
coarse salt, such as kosher

Pesto Sauce
1 cup prepared basil pesto sauce

directions preheat oven to 400°

To prepare the focaccia, dissolve the yeast and sugar in 1 cup of the lukewarm water in a bowl and let it sit until the mixture is frothy. In another bowl, add the remaining ¾ cup water, the olive oil and the table salt. Pour in the yeast mixture. Blend in the flour, 1 cup at a time, until the dough comes together. Knead the dough on a floured board for 10 minutes, adding flour as needed to make the dough smooth and elastic. Place the dough in an oiled bowl, turn to coat evenly, and cover with a towel. Let the dough rise in a warm place for 1 hour, until it doubles in size.

Punch down the dough and knead for 5 minutes. Gently roll out the dough to fit a 15x10 baking pan. Let it rise for 15 minutes, covered. Oil your fingers and make slight impressions in the dough, 1 inch apart. Let rise for 1 hour.

Drizzle the dough with olive oil and sprinkle with the coarse salt. Bake for 20 minutes at 400° until golden brown. Sprinkle with additional oil if desired.

To prepare the vegetables, pour the vinegar into a large mixing bowl, then slowly add the olive oil, whisking quickly. Whisk in the thyme, oregano, lemon juice, garlic, salt and pepper. Add the vegetables and toss lightly. Cover the bowl and marinate for 1 hour.

Heat a barbecue or indoor grill. Shape a large roasting pan with aluminum foil, turning up the edges. Remove the vegetables from the marinade and place in the foil pan. Save the vinegar mixture. Grill the vegetables, turning once, for approximately 15 minutes, or until they are slightly firm to the bite. Remove them from the grill, put them back in the bowl with the vinaigrette, and lightly toss.

To prepare the sandwiches, slice the cooled focaccia in half and spread the bottom half with pesto sauce. Remove the vegetables from the vinegar mixture and arrange on top of the pesto. Place the top half of the focaccia on the vegetables and cut into 8 pieces.

pair with thumbprint cellars syrah and cabernet sauvignon

pasta & rice

Clos du Bois Wines

19410 geyserville avenue, geyserville, ca 95441
707-857-3100

www.closdubois.com

(Ragu Bolognese, a meat sauce, is a specialty of the Bologna region
of northeastern Italy. Serve it with cooked pasta such as tagliatelle
and pappardelle—flat, wide ribbons to which the hearty sauce clings
nicely. Instead of spooning the sauce over the pasta, add the cooked
pasta to the sauce and toss to coat evenly. **Serves 10 to 12**)

ragu bolognese

chef Rick Bidia

ingredients

¼ cup extra virgin olive oil
4 tablespoons unsalted butter
2 medium onions, finely chopped
4 stalks celery, finely chopped
1 carrot, scraped and finely chopped
5 cloves garlic, sliced
1 pound ground veal
1 pound ground pork
½ pound ground beef
¼ pound pancetta, minced
5 cans (16-ounce) peeled crushed tomatoes, with the juices
1-½ cups Clos du Bois Cabernet Sauvignon

kosher salt to taste
black pepper to taste
Parmigiano-Reggiano cheese, for grating

directions

In a 6- to 8-quart, heavy-bottom saucepan, heat the olive oil and butter over medium heat. Add the onions, celery, carrot and garlic, and cook over medium heat until the vegetables are translucent. Add the veal, pork, beef and pancetta to the pan and brown over high heat for 15 to 20 minutes, stirring to keep the meat from sticking together.

Add the tomatoes and simmer for 15 minutes. Add the wine, bring to a boil, lower the heat and simmer for 2 to 2-½ hours, until the flavors are developed. Remove from the heat and season with salt and pepper to taste. Toss the sauce and pasta and top with freshly grated Parmigiano-Reggiano cheese.

pair with clos du bois alexander valley cabernet sauvignon

Korbel Champagne Cellars

13250 river road, guerneville, ca 95446
707-824-7000

www.korbel.com

If you don't have preserved lemons in your pantry, they're easy to
make, although the process takes two weeks. When preserved,
the lemons will keep for up to six months in cold storage; use
them with roast chicken, Moroccan stews, sautéed greens,
roasted vegetables and in melted butter for dipping artichokes.
They add a fresh, bright flavor to these risotto cakes. **Serves 8**

risotto cakes

with fresh thyme and preserved lemon
chef Robin Lehnhoff McCray

ingredients

Preserved Lemons

10 lemons
2 to 3 cups kosher salt
1 tablespoon red pepper flakes
2 bay leaves
1 tablespoon black peppercorns
1 cinnamon stick
4 cups fresh lemon juice

Risotto Cakes

2 tablespoons extra virgin olive oil
4 tablespoons onion, minced
1 tablespoon garlic, minced
Salt and pepper to taste
1 cup Arborio rice
4 cups chicken stock, boiling
1 cup grated dry jack cheese
2 tablespoons fresh thyme leaves
2 tablespoons preserved lemon, minced

directions to prepare the lemons, start 2 weeks ahead

Cut the lemons in half and rub the cut surfaces with kosher salt. Place the lemon halves into a gallon-size sterile jar. Add all the other ingredients except the lemon juice. Pour the remaining salt over the lemons and then add all the lemon juice. Store in the refrigerator and shake the jar daily for 2 weeks. When ready to use each lemon, rinse off the salt and remove the flesh and pith, leaving only the peel.

To prepare the risotto cakes, preheat the oven to 325°. Heat the olive oil in a 4-quart, heavy-bottom pot. Sauté the onion and garlic until soft, then season with salt and pepper. Add the rice and stir constantly for 3 to 5 minutes. Slowly add ½ cup of stock at a time to the rice, stirring as it cooks, until all 4 cups have been added. Al dente risotto takes between 15 and 18 minutes to cook, so don't rush.

Add the remaining ingredients and set aside to cool completely.

Use a 4-ounce scoop to make risotto balls, then gently flatten each ball with the palm of your hand. Heat a sauté pan that has been lightly coated with olive oil. When very hot, sear the cakes on both sides to a light golden-brown color. Remove the cakes from the pan and keep them warm in the preheated oven until ready to serve.

pair with korbel natural champagne

Lynmar Winery

3909 frei road, sebastopol, ca 95472
707-829-3374

www.lynmarwinery.com

(I developed this recipe for our 2007 industry hospitality party, to go with grilled pork tenderloin, and paired it with Lynmar Pinot Noir. I wanted a side dish rich in texture to highlight the richness of the wine, and something earthy to act as a counterpoint to the Pinot Noir's elegant fruit. This is an easy recipe to make and it can be doubled or tripled to feed a crowd. Much of the flavor comes from the Sottocenere al Tartufo, a semi-soft cow's milk cheese that has bits of black truffle in it; you'll find it at specialty cheese shops. **10 side-dish servings**)

truffle mac & cheese

chef Sandra Simile

ingredients

2 cups penne pasta
3 tablespoons butter
2 tablespoons white flour
½ cup sweet onion, minced (Vidalia or Walla Walla)
2 teaspoons fresh lemon thyme, minced
½ teaspoon ground black pepper
1 teaspoon kosher salt
2-¼ cups whole milk
2-½ cups Sottocenere al Tartufo cheese, grated
1 tablespoon olive oil
½ cup panko Japanese bread crumbs

directions preheat oven to 350°

Cook the penne in 1 gallon of salted water until al dente, slightly firm to the bite. Drain the pasta and place it in a large bowl. Set aside.

Melt 2 tablespoons of the butter in a 2-quart saucepan over medium heat. When the butter starts to foam, add the flour, stirring with a whisk, and cook for 1 minute. Add the onion, lemon thyme, pepper and salt and continue to cook, stirring constantly, for 2 minutes. Slowly whisk in the milk. Simmer gently, stirring often, for about 12 minutes.

Remove the pan from the heat and immediately add the contents to the bowl of pasta. Add the grated cheese and blend well. Place the mixture in a greased, 1½- to 2-quart baking dish.

Melt the olive oil and the remaining 1 tablespoon of butter in a small skillet. Add the bread crumbs and stir well. Sprinkle the crumbs on top of the casserole and bake in the oven for 30 minutes. Let stand 5 to 10 minutes before serving.

pair with lynmar pinot noir

White Oak Vineyards & Winery

7505 highway 128, healdsburg, ca 95448
707-433-8429

www.whiteoakwinery.com

A few years ago, Bill Myers, owner of White Oak, had a bumper crop of heirloom tomatoes from his garden at the winery. We made a delicious tomato sauce and froze it for later use. Later that fall, after a long day of crushing grapes, we took the sauce out of the freezer and whipped up a satisfying meal to feed everyone. This dish is what the pantry yielded, and it has become a staff favorite. **Serves 6 to 8**

pasta & rice

radiatore

with sausage and peas
chef Janet Saleby

ingredients

2 tablespoons extra virgin olive oil
½ pound hot Italian sausage, casings removed
2 garlic cloves, minced
1 small shallot, minced
2-½ cups prepared tomato sauce (from your garden, if available)
¼ cup White Oak Syrah
¼ cup heavy cream
½ cup frozen baby peas
salt to taste
1 pound radiatore pasta
½ cup Parmigiano-Reggiano cheese, freshly grated
2 tablespoons basil, freshly shredded

directions

In a large saucepan, heat the olive oil. Add the sausage and cook over moderately high heat, breaking up the meat into small pieces with a wooden spoon, until lightly browned, about 8 minutes. Add the minced garlic and shallot and cook, stirring, until softened, about 2 minutes. Add the tomato sauce and bring to a simmer.

Partially cover the saucepan and cook the sauce over low heat for 30 minutes. Stir in the Syrah, then the cream and still-frozen peas, and simmer over low heat for 10 minutes. Season to taste with salt.

Meanwhile, cook the pasta in boiling salted water until al dente, with just a slight resistance to the bite. Drain and return the pasta to the pot. Add the tomato sauce and ¼ cup of the Parmigiano-Reggiano and toss over low heat until the pasta absorbs some of the sauce. Transfer the pasta to bowls and top with the remaining cheese and the basil.

pair with white oak syrah

entrées

Acorn Winery/Alegria Vineyards

12040 old redwood highway, healdsburg, ca 95448
707-433-6440

www.acornwinery.com

Acorn squash and Acorn Sangiovese – a match made in Russian River Valley heaven. This sumptuous chicken dish is enhanced by the addition of acorn squash and makes for a satisfying fall and winter supper. We like to serve it on a bed of creamy polenta. **Serves 6**

chicken cacciatore

with acorn squash

chef Jeff Mall, Chef/Owner, Zin Restaurant & Wine Bar

ingredients

4 pounds chicken thighs
kosher salt and fresh ground black pepper
¼ cup red wine vinegar
¼ cup olive oil
½ cup bacon, diced
4 cups yellow onion, diced
4 cloves garlic, sliced
1 acorn squash, peeled and diced
1 pound crimini mushrooms, wiped cleaned and sliced
1 tablespoon fresh thyme, chopped
2 teaspoons fresh rosemary, chopped
1 28-ounce can Italian tomatoes, chopped
½ cup Acorn Sangiovese
2 cups chicken stock
½ cup oil-cured black olives, pitted
½ cup Italian parsley, chopped

directions

In a large bowl, add the chicken and season with kosher salt and black pepper. Add the red wine vinegar and toss. Marinate the chicken in the vinegar for 1 hour, then remove and pat the thighs dry with a paper towel.

Pour the olive oil into a large sauté pan and warm over medium heat. Add the bacon and cook until it's brown. Add the marinated chicken, skin side down, and brown each thigh on both sides. Use a slotted spoon to remove the bacon and chicken from the pan, and set the meat aside. Drain off half of the fat from the pan.

Add the onion, garlic, squash and mushrooms to the same pan. Cook over medium heat for 5 minutes, or until the onions are translucent. Add the thyme, rosemary, tomatoes, Sangiovese and chicken stock, and bring to a boil.

Add the chicken and bacon back to the pan, cover, and reduce the heat to low. Simmer for 30 minutes. Remove the lid, add the olives and parsley, and cook 5 minutes more. Skim the fat from the surface of the sauce and season the sauce to taste with kosher salt and pepper. Serve on top of soft polenta.

pair with acorn alegria vineyards russian river valley sangiovese

Alderbrook Winery

2306 magnolia drive, healdsburg, ca 95448
707-433-5987

www.alderbrook.com

Other than vegetarians, who doesn't love a
bacon cheeseburger? This recipe expands on
the all-American classic, using aged cheddar for
more depth of flavor, and spicing things up with
a tangy Zinfandel barbecue sauce. **Serves 4**

mini bacon burgers

with aged cheddar and alderbrook zinfandel barbecue sauce

chef Dan Lucci

ingredients

Barbecue Sauce

2 tablespoons olive oil
½ cup onion, diced
1 cup Alderbrook Zinfandel
⅓ cup orange juice
3 tablespoons apple cider vinegar
1 cup ketchup
⅓ cup dark molasses
4 tablespoons brown sugar

Burgers

8 small hamburger buns, toasted
2 pounds ground chuck, divided into 8 patties
½ pound dry-cured bacon, cooked and sliced thin
kosher salt and pepper
8 slices aged cheddar cheese

directions

To prepare the barbecue sauce, heat the olive oil and sauté the onion for 5 minutes. Add the Zinfandel and cook until the volume is reduce by half. Add the orange juice, vinegar, ketchup and molasses. Cook for 20 minutes or until thick.

To prepare the burgers, heat a gas grill to medium-high, or prepare a medium-hot charcoal fire. Season the 8 hamburger patties with salt and pepper and grill to desired doneness. Toast the buns on the grill. Spread 1 tablespoon of the barbecue sauce on the bottom half of each bun, then add a patty, a slice of cheddar and a slice of bacon. Top with the remaining bun half.

pair with alderbrook zinfandel

Alexander Valley Vineyards

8644 highway 128, healdsburg, ca 95448
707-433-7209

www.avvwine.com

This recipe honors Margaret Cranford Kirkpatrick Wetzel, who with her husband, Harry, founded Alexander Valley Vineyards in 1962. "Maggie" passed away in May 2008 at age 83, but not before she shared many of her culinary ideas with our chef, Jeff Young. Maggie came home one summer from a vacation in Italy and gave Jeff the inspiration for this dish. Demi-glace, a prepared brown sauce made from veal stock, and mushroom essence can be found in gourmet markets and some large supermarkets. **Serves 2**

pork shanks

with tuscan beans

chef Jeff Young

ingredients

Pork Shanks

2 tablespoons oil
2 fresh pork shanks
3 carrots, peeled and chopped
4 celery stalks, chopped
2 yellow onions, chopped
4 leeks, chopped and washed
  (white and light green parts only)
8 cloves garlic, smashed
1 tablespoon fennel seeds
1 tablespoon cumin seeds
salt and pepper
1 tablespoon smoked paprika

1 tablespoon demi-glace
1 teaspoon mushroom essence
1-½ quarts water
¼ cup olive oil
1 onion, minced
6 cloves garlic, minced
1 teaspoon fresh thyme, chopped
1 teaspoon fresh sage, chopped
1 teaspoon fresh oregano, chopped
14 ounces reserved pork stock
1 pound dry cannellini beans, soaked overnight,
  drained, cooked in a large pot until tender, then drained

Gremolata

2 anchovy filets
1 tablespoon parsley, chopped
1 Meyer lemon, zest and juice

directions start the pork shanks and the beans 1 day ahead

To prepare the pork shanks, heat a large sauté pan on medium-high heat. Add the 2 tablespoons of oil and brown the shanks on all sides. Remove them to a large oven-proof pan. Add the carrots, celery, onions, leeks and garlic and cook for 5 minutes. Add the fennel, cumin, salt, pepper and paprika, and cook for 2 more minutes.

Add the demi-glace, mushroom essence and water and bring to a boil. Pour the liquid over the shanks and cover the pan tightly. Place the pan in a 375° oven and cook for 3 hours. Remove the shanks from the oven and place them on a plate to cool. Strain the remaining pork liquid and refrigerate overnight. When the pork is cool enough to handle, remove and discard the skin. Remove the meat from the bone in large pieces and refrigerate overnight.

The next day, remove the pork stock from the refrigerator and skim off the fat from the surface. Remove the shank meat from the refrigerator. In a large sauté pan, add the ¼ cup oil and sauté the minced onion until it's soft. Add the garlic and herbs and cook for 2 minutes. Add the reserved pork stock and bring to a boil, then add the meat and cooked beans. Cover and cook for 45 minutes, or until tender.

Right before serving, make the gremolata by chopping together the anchovies, parsley and lemon zest. Mix in the lemon juice and pour the gremolata over the pork. Serve in large bowls with crusty French bread.

pair with alexander valley vineyards estate syrah

Arista Winery

7015 westside road, healdsburg, ca 95448
707-473-0606

www.aristawinery.com

"Arista di Maiale" is roast loin of pork with rosemary. It's a fabulous match for Arista Russian River Valley Pinot Noir. **Serves 12**

arista di maiale

"roast of pork loin with rosemary"

chef Janis McWilliams

ingredients

1 bone-in pork loin, 4 to 5 pounds
leaves from 4 fresh rosemary sprigs
6 garlic cloves
salt and pepper, to taste
¼ cup olive oil
2 ounces (½ stick) unsalted butter
1 medium yellow onion, coarsely chopped
½ cup dry white wine (preferably Arista Sauvignon Blanc)

directions preheat oven to 350°

Have the butcher remove the chine bone from the pork loin, or break the bone to make carving easier. Trim off the excess fat from the pork but keep some in place. Using a very sharp knife, cut about 12 small slits in the pork, making some very deep, some shallow, and some in-between cuts.

Chop together the rosemary and garlic. Transfer to a small bowl and stir in a little salt and pepper. The moisture from the garlic should hold the seasonings together; if not, add a bit of olive oil. Insert a small amount of this mixture into each slit in the pork, using your fingertip to push the mixture to the bottom of the slit.

Put the butter in a shallow roasting pan and place in the oven until melted. Sprinkle the onion on top of the melted butter. Place the pork loin directly on top of the onion; do not use a roasting rack. Drizzle a small amount of olive oil over the pork and add the wine to the pan. Roast, uncovered, basting with the wine about every 20 minutes, until an instant-read thermometer registers 170°, about 2 to 2-½ hours. Transfer the pork to a carving board and let it rest for 10 to 15 minutes before carving.

pair with arista russian river valley pinot noir

Battaglini Estate Winery

2948 piner road, santa rosa, ca 95401
707-578-4091

www.battagliniwines.com

This recipe was first served to winery owner Joe Battaglini
by his grandmother in Altopascio, Italy. The chicken used in
the dish served to Joe was the same chicken his children
saw roaming around the farm that morning. Of course, the
kids did not learn this until many years later. **Serves 6**

entrées

chicken cacciatore

chef Lucia Battaglini

ingredients

¼ cup olive oil
3 pounds skinless, boneless chicken, cut into cubes
salt and pepper
1 medium onion, diced
3 cloves garlic, minced
3 tablespoons fresh sage, or 1 teaspoon dried
¾ cup Chardonnay
1 large red or green bell pepper (or both), cut into strips
3 large tomatoes, peeled and cut into wedges, or 1 32-ounce can peeled, diced tomatoes

directions

In a large sauté pan, heat the olive oil. Add the chicken and season with salt and pepper. Cook the chicken, turning frequently, until almost brown on all sides. Add the onion, garlic and sage, stir, and continue to cook until the chicken is browned.

Add the wine and the green and/or red peppers. Sauté for a few minutes, then add the tomatoes. Simmer uncovered until the chicken is cooked, about 30 minutes. Add more wine if needed to keep the chicken moist. Do not overcook. Serve hot.

pair with battaglini zinfandel and petite sirah

Bella Vineyards & Wine Caves

9711 west dry creek road, healdsburg, ca 95448
707-473-9171

www.bellawinery.com

This Italian-inspired lamb dish is very easy to make, yet delivers big, hearty flavor. Santi executive chef Dino Bugica suggests accompanying the lamb with braised Romano beans or sautéed greens. **Serves 6**

braised lamb

chef Dino Bugica, Executive Chef, Taverna Santi

ingredients

¼ cup olive oil
2 pounds lamb shoulder, cubed
1 white onion, diced
2 stalks celery, chopped
1 carrot, chopped
1 bottle (750ml) Bella Lily Hill Zinfandel
1 cup vegetable stock
2 sprigs rosemary
salt and pepper to taste

directions preheat oven to 250°

In a heavy-bottomed pot, heat the oil over medium-high heat. Sear the lamb cubes, making sure to brown them on all sides. Remove the lamb from the pan and set aside.

Add the onion to the pan and sauté until it's translucent. Add the celery and carrot, and sauté until the vegetables begin to caramelize. Stir in the wine, vegetable stock and rosemary and heat through. Transfer the liquid to a baking dish and add the seared lamb to the dish. Season with salt and pepper. Cover the dish with foil and cook for 2 hours.

When the meat is tender, remove it from the oven and pour the braising liquid into a large saucepan. Heat the liquid over medium heat until it reduces to a thick sauce. Add the lamb to the reduced liquid and season to taste.

pair with bella lily hill zinfandel

Carol Shelton Wines

3354-B coffey lane, santa rosa, ca 95403
707-575-3441

www.carolshelton.com

We first served this delicious stew at Winter Wineland 2008. After tasting our Monga Zin, Stella's' chef Greg Hallihan created this combination of exciting flavors to showcase the spiciness of our wine. The original stew took two days to create, and nearly three months to duplicate, as Greg often works without benefit of recipes. **Serves 8**

moroccan pork stew

chef Greg Hallihan, Stella's at Russian River Vineyards

ingredients

Dry Rub

8 ounces ground cumin
1 tablespoon cayenne pepper
1 tablespoon ground cinnamon
3 tablespoons kosher or sea salt

Pork Stew

4 pounds pork pillows (pork butt will do but pillows are leaner)
4 tablespoons oil
6 quarts chicken stock
4 large carrots, diced
4 large onions, diced
1 large jalapeno chile, diced
8 cloves garlic, minced
1 cup couscous
4 ounces fresh ginger, grated
1 tablespoon turmeric, ground
2 bunches cilantro, chopped

directions

To prepare the dry rub, in a small bowl, combine the cumin, cayenne, cinnamon and salt.

To prepare the stew, using your hands, generously rub the spices into the pork. In a large, heavy-bottomed pot, heat the oil over medium-high heat and sear the pork until it's nicely brown on all sides. Add to the pot enough chicken stock to cover the meat. Reduce the heat to medium, cover the pot and simmer the pork for 2 hours.

After the pork has been braised, reserve the liquid. Remove the pork from the pot and cut it into 1-inch cubes. In the same pot, sauté all the remaining ingredients except for the cilantro, then pour in the braising liquid. Increase the heat to a simmer, add the pork, and let simmer for 20 minutes. Add half of the chopped cilantro and let simmer another 5 minutes. Season with salt and serve in bowls, garnished with the remaining cilantro.

pair with carol shelton monga zin

C. Donatiello Winery

4035 westside road, healdsburg, ca 95448
707-431-4442

www.cdonatiello.com

At Zazu, we like to play with American classics, so the
cooking is familiar and comforting, yet also challenging
and fun. We love C. Donatiello's Pinot Noir with local
rabbit—and truffles, of course. You can substitute all
chicken or duck legs for the rabbit in this recipe. **Serves 8**

cloverdale rabbit
shepherd's pie
with truffled mashed potato topper
chefs Duskie Estes and John Stewart, Zazu and Bovolo

ingredients

Rabbit

2 rabbits, cut into 8 pieces each
4 chicken legs, with thighs attached
olive oil for sauteeing
3 ribs celery, roughly chopped
2 onions, roughly chopped
2 carrots, roughly chopped
2 bay leaves
1 bottle C. Donatiello Pinot Noir
6 cups chicken stock
kosher salt and black pepper to taste

Truffled Mashed Potato Topper

3 pounds russet potatoes, peeled and quartered
3 pounds Yukon Gold potatoes, cut in half
1-1/3 cups buttermilk
10 tablespoons unsalted butter
¾ cup sour cream
1-½ teaspoons white truffle oil, or to taste
kosher salt and black pepper to taste

Additional Components

3 cups snap peas, cut on the bias, ¼-inch thick
3 cups carrots, peeled and cut in half lengthwise, then into
¼-inch-thick half moons
3 tablespoons freshly grated Parmesan cheese

directions preheat oven to 325°

To prepare the rabbit, season it and the chicken pieces with salt and pepper. In a large straight-sided sauté pan, heat the olive oil and brown the meat on both sides, about 7 minutes. Remove from the pan and set aside. In the same pan, add the celery, onions and carrots and sauté until they start to brown, about 3 minutes. Add the bay leaves, Pinot Noir and meat pieces to the pan. Let simmer for a few minutes. Add the stock, cover the pan, place it in the oven and cook at 325° until the meat begins to fall off the bone, about 1 hour. Remove the meat from the oven and then from the braising liquid. Cool slightly and pick the meat off the bones. Strain the braising liquid to remove the solids, skim to remove any fat, and reserve.

To prepare the potato topping, in a large pot, place the potatoes, 2 teaspoons of salt and enough cold water to cover. Bring to a boil over high heat. Reduce the heat and cook the potatoes until tender, about 20 minutes. Drain through a food mill. Mill and fold in the buttermilk, butter, sour cream and truffle oil. Season with salt and pepper. Set aside.

To prepare the additional filling, heat a large saucepan on high and blanch the snap peas, then shock them in an ice water bath. Do the same with the carrots. To assemble the pie, heat the oven to 375°. In an oven-proof dish, distribute the rabbit and chicken meat, peas, carrots and 1-½ cups of the reserved braising liquid. If you don't have enough liquid, use chicken stock. Top with the mashed potatoes. Generously sprinkle with Parmesan. Bake until hot throughout, about 30 minutes.

If the top is not golden, switch on the broiler feature and brown for a few minutes.

pair with c. donatiello pinot noir

Chalk Hill Estate Vineyards & Winery

10300 chalk hill road, healdsburg, ca 95448
707-838-4306

www.chalkhill.com

Tomato concassé (kon-kah-SAY) is the French culinary term
for tomatoes that have had all the skin, seeds and core
removed from them, then are chopped. This recipe calls for
1 quart of tomato concassé; depending on the juiciness of
your tomatoes, 4 pounds should be enough for this dish.
The bamboo skewers are for presentation only, so there is
no need to soak them in water ahead of time. **Serves 6**

sweet and sour
swordfish skewers

chef Didier Ageorges, Executive Chef, Chalk Hill Estate

ingredients

Tomato Concassé
4 pounds ripe red tomatoes

Swordfish
5 tablespoons olive oil
5 whole garlic cloves
1 pound swordfish loin, cut into 1-inch cubes
1 32-ounce can tomato sauce
1 quart tomato concassé
4 tablespoons capers
1 tablespoon cumin powder
4 tablespoons red wine vinegar
2 tablespoons honey
Worcestershire sauce
12 bamboo skewers

directions

To prepare the tomato concassé, with a small paring knife, cut a small "X" in the bottom of the tomatoes and drop them into a pot of boiling water for about 30 seconds, until the skin begins to lift at the X score. Remove the tomatoes to a bowl of ice water to stop the cooking. Peel off all the skin, gently squeeze the tomatoes to remove the core and seeds, using a teaspoon to get to pockets of seeds. Chop into small dice.

To prepare the swordfish, in a sauté pan over high heat, heat the oil, add the garlic, and pan-sear the fish cubes until they are just tender. This will take approximately 2 minutes. Set aside the fish in a glass baking dish.

In the same pan, combine the tomato sauce, concassé, capers, cumin, red wine vinegar, honey and Worchestershire sauce, and cook over medium heat for approximately 5 minutes. Pour the seasoning over the fish. Let cool. To serve, thread the fish cubes on 12 bamboo skewers.

pair with chalk hill estate sauvignon blanc

Davis Family Vineyards

52 front street, healdsburg, ca 95448
707-433-3858

www.daviswines.com

Spit-roasted pig is definitely party pork; a 50-pound pig serves between 25 and 50 people, depending on the amount of other fixins'. Allow 1 to 2 pounds of pig weight per person. Marinate the pig at least 1 day and up to 3 days in advance of roasting. We love to use Guy Davis' Apple-ation apple brandy in the marinade and the braised cabbage side dish; it's such a clear expression of our West County apples.

spit-roasted pig

with apple-ation-braised cabbage

chefs Duskie Estes and John Stewart, Zazu and Bovolo

ingredients

Pig and Marinade

1 350ml bottle Davis Family Apple-ation apple brandy
2 cups olive oil
2 cups apple cider
2 cups apple cider vinegar
3 onions, roughly chopped
4 cinnamon sticks
1 tablespoon whole cloves
2 tablespoons allspice
1 tablespoon red pepper flakes
kosher salt and freshly ground black pepper to taste
1 50- to 80-pound pig

Apple-ation-Braised Cabbage

6 tablespoons unsalted butter
2 apples, grated
1 onion, julienned
1 head green cabbage, cut into wide chiffonade
¼ cup Apple-ation apple brandy
¼ cup apple cider
¼ cup chicken stock
kosher salt and black pepper to taste

directions marinate the pig 1 to 3 days before roasting

To prepare the pig, combine all the marinade ingredients. Score the skin with a sharp knife, place the pig in the marinade and let it sit, refrigerated, for 1 to 3 days.

The heat on the rotisserie should be indirect and you should build a hotter fire near the hams and a smaller fire near the loins. Have a spray bottle of water available to put out any flare-ups. Baste every hour with the marinade. Bring to an internal temperature of 145°, and let rest about ½ hour before butchering. (It will climb to 155°). The cooking time will take somewhere between 4 to 8 hours, depending on the weight of the pig; a 50- to 80-pound pig will take approximately 4 to 5 hours.

To prepare the braised cabbage, preheat the oven to 350°. In a large oven-proof sauté pan, melt the butter over medium heat and sauté the apples and onion until fragrant. Add the cabbage and sauté until the mixture just starts to turn brown, about 5 minutes. Add the brandy, cider and stock. Sprinkle with salt and pepper. Cover the pan with foil and braise the cabbage in the oven until tender, about 1 hour. Season wiith salt and pepper. Serves 6 and can be multiplied.

pair with davis family pinot noir and riesling

DeLoach Vineyards

1791 olivet road, santa rosa, ca 95401
707-526-9111

www.deloachvineyards.com

For the wine ingredient in this dish, DeLoach culinary director Cyndicy Coudray likes to use the wine she plans to serve with the meal. She suggests Pinot Noir or Zinfandel here, yet DeLoach Merlot and Cabernet Sauvignon would work just as well in the recipe and at the table. Serve these melt-in-your-mouth ribs over egg noodles. **Serves 6**

savory beef short ribs

with olives

chef Cyndicy Coudray, Culinary Director, DeLoach Vineyards

ingredients

Marinade

3 cups DeLoach Vineyards Pinot Noir or Zinfandel
1-½ tablespoons garlic, minced
2 bay leaves
1 tablespoon fresh rosemary, stemmed and chopped
1 tablespoon fresh thyme, stemmed and chopped
2 3-inch strips orange zest, removed with a vegetable peeler
1 teaspoon ground pepper

Ribs

5-½ to 6 pounds beef short ribs
¼ cup olive oil
2 large onions, chopped
2 celery ribs, chopped
2 carrots, chopped
1 cup drained Kalamata olives, pitted
2 cups beef stock
½ cup freshly squeezed orange juice
3 tablespoons flat leaf parsley, chopped
fresh rosemary for garnish

directions marinate the ribs 1 day in advance

In a large bowl, combine all the marinade ingredients. Trim the excess fat from the ribs and place them in a large glass baking dish. Pour the marinade over the ribs, cover with plastic wrap and place in the refrigerator overnight.

When you're ready to cook the ribs, preheat the oven to 350°. Remove ribs from the marinade and pat them dry with paper towels. Remove the orange zest and bay leaves and discard, reserving the marinade. Heat the oil in a large skillet over medium heat and brown the ribs on all sides. Place them in a shallow roasting pan.

In the same skillet, sauté the onions, celery and carrots for 5 minutes. Add the olives, warm through, and transfer to the roasting pan. Deglaze the skillet with marinade, add the beef stock, and pour over the meat and vegetables. Cover and bake for 2½ hours or until tender. Adjust the seasonings and serve over egg noodles.

pair with deloach vineyards pinot noir and zinfandel

Dutton Estate & Sebastopol Vineyards

8757 green valley road, sebastopol, ca 95472
707-829-9463

duttonestate.com

Succulent, spiced pulled pork is a slow-cooked, hearty dish for fall and winter. It's great for a party or a big meal, as it can be prepared ahead and kept warm in a slow cooker, ready to be piled onto buns, polenta or cornbread. In this recipe, the pork is combined with a hot and spicy blackberry and orange chipotle sauce created by Carol Kozlowski, Tracy Dutton's mother. **Serves 6**

oven-roasted pulled pork

with blackberry and orange chipotle sauce

chef Cynthia Newcomb

ingredients

Pork Roast

1 pork butt roast, 5 to 6 pounds
2 teaspoons smoked paprika
2 teaspoons celery salt
1 teaspoon kosher or sea salt
1 teaspoon black pepper, coarse ground
1 teaspoon cumin powder
1 tablespoon brown sugar
1 teaspoon dried sage
2 tablespoons mustard (yellow or Dijon)

Blackberry & Orange Chipotle Sauce

1 10-ounce jar Kozlowski Farms blackberry jam
1 10-ounce jar Kozlowski Farms orange marmalade
$1/3$ cup Kozlowski Farms black raspberry vinegar
$1/2$ cup Dutton Estate Syrah
$1/4$ cup canned chipotle peppers in adobo sauce
1 teaspoon kosher or sea salt

directions season the pork and refrigerate 1 day ahead

Trim the pork roast of excess fat. In a small bowl, combine all the dry ingredients. Slather the roast with the mustard to moisten. Coat the roast with the dry mixture, cover with plastic wrap and refrigerate overnight. Remove the roast from the refrigerator an hour before roasting and bring to room temperature.

To prepare the sauce, in a non-stick saucepan, warm the jam and marmalade over low heat. In a blender, add the vinegar, wine, chipotles with adobo sauce and salt. Blend until smooth. Add the mixture to the jam and marmalade, bring to a boil, and turn down the heat until the sauce is just simmering. Simmer 8 to 10 minutes.

Preheat the oven to 300°. Put the pork on a rack in a foil-lined roasting pan and tent the foil to cover. Bake for 6 to 7 hours, removing the foil for the last hour. The meat is done when a fork inserted in the meat can be twisted. An instant-read thermometer inserted in the thickest part of the pork should register 170°. Remove the meat from the oven and let it rest at least 30 minutes before "pulling". Shred the pork, making sure to incorporate the crunchy bits throughout. Combine the meat with 2 cups of the sauce, or more to taste, and serve.

pair with dutton estate syrah

Ferrari-Carano Vineyards & Winery

8761 dry creek road, healdsburg, ca 95448
707-433-6700

www.ferrari-carano.com

When combined with butter, the juice from roasted lemons gives the sea bass an extraordinary depth of flavor. Fennel baked in the oven provides a savory bed for the fish. **Serves 4**

sea bass

with caramelized fennel and roasted lemon butter

chef Rhonda Carano

ingredients

3 whole lemons, scrubbed and washed
½ teaspoon sugar
½ cup fish stock or chicken broth
salt and ground black pepper
1 pinch cayenne pepper
8 tablespoons unsalted butter
3 tablespoons olive oil
2 large fennel bulbs, cut into thin slices; reserve green tops
4 6-ounce sea bass fillets
salt and pepper
spring of thyme

directions preheat oven to 375°

Place the lemons on aluminum foil and sprinkle with sugar and 2 tablespoons of water. Fold the foil over the lemons, seal tightly and roast on a cookie sheet for 35 to 40 minutes, or until the lemons are soft. Let the lemons cool to the touch. Cut them in half and squeeze the juice into a small saucepan. Stir in the stock and bring to a boil. Skim the liquid and season with salt, pepper and cayenne. Add the butter, a small piece at a time, whisking constantly. Keep warm.

Increase the oven temperature to 425°. Heat 2 tablespoons of the olive oil in a roasting pan. Add the fennel and cook without stirring, until the fennel starts to brown. Set the pan in the oven and roast the fennel for 30 minutes, or until tender.

When the fennel is almost done, prepare the fish. Season the bass on both sides with salt and pepper. Heat the remaining 1 tablespoon of oil in a large oven-proof sauté pan until hot. Place the fillets in the pan and sear for 2 to 3 minutes per side. Place the pan in the oven and roast for 5 minutes, or until the fish is just cooked through.

Remove the fennel from the oven and arrange on each of 4 serving plates. Place a bass fillet on top of the fennel. Ladle 2 ounces of the lemon butter around each fillet and garnish with the reserved green fennel tops and thyme. Serve immediately.

pair with with ferrari-carano tre terre chardonnay

Forchini Vineyards & Winery

5141 dry creek road, healdsburg, ca 95448
707-431-8886

www.forchini.com

Goulash is the ultimate comfort food in Hungary, Austria and Germany. Typically served with homemade noodles, called spaetzle, goulash is equally delicious over fluffy mashed potatoes. With a crusty loaf of bread, tossed green salad and Forchini wine, you will have a memorable winter meal. **Serves 4**

hearty hungarian

goulash

chef Randi Kauppi, Oui Cater

ingredients

1-½ pounds onions, chopped
1 whole garlic bulb, minced
1-½ cups butter
1-½ cups olive oil
2 pounds beef, cut into cubes
salt and pepper to taste
1 red and yellow pepper, thinly sliced
1-½ tablespoons Hungarian paprika
1 cup cherry tomatoes
1 quart beef stock
1 cup Forchini Zinfandel
3 bay leaves
1 teaspoon thyme

directions

In a medium stock pot, sauté the onions and garlic in ⅓ of the butter and olive oil until golden. In a large frying pan, heat the remainder of the butter and oil and lightly brown the beef cubes, sprinkling with salt and pepper. Add the beef to the onion mixture, along with the peppers, paprika, tomatoes, beef stock, wine, bay leaves and thyme. Simmer with the lid ajar for 1-½ to 2 hours, or until the beef is tender. Serve over hot, buttered noodles or mashed potatoes.

pair with forchini old vine zinfandel, beausierra bordeaux blend and papa nonno tuscan red

Fritz Underground Winery

24691 dutcher creek road, cloverdale, ca 95425
707-894-3389

www.fritzwinery.com

Beef Bourguignon is a traditional French dish in which beef and vegetables are braised in red wine. In Bourgogne (Burgundy), Pinot Noir is the cooking wine of choice, though at Fritz, we love it with Cabernet Sauvignon, which gives the stew a heartier flavor. **Serves 6**

beef bourguignon

chef Natalia Fritz

ingredients

1 tablespoon olive oil
8 ounces dry-cured, center-cut applewood
  smoked bacon, diced
2-½ pounds beef chuck, cut into 1-inch cubes
kosher salt
black pepper
1 pound carrots, sliced diagonally into
  1-inch chunks
2 yellow onions, sliced
2 cloves garlic, chopped
½ cup Cognac or other brandy
1-½ cups Fritz Cabernet Sauvignon
3-½ cups beef broth

1 tablespoon tomato paste
1 teaspoon fresh thyme leaves, or ½ teaspoon dried
4 tablespoons unsalted butter at room
  temperature, divided
3 tablespoons all-purpose flour
1 pound frozen whole pearl onions
1 pound mushrooms, stems discarded and caps
  thickly sliced
sourdough or country bread, sliced
1 whole garlic clove, peeled

directions preheat oven to 250°

In a large Dutch oven, heat the olive oil over medium heat. Add the bacon and cook for
10 minutes, stirring occasionally, until the bacon is lightly browned. Remove the bacon with
a slotted spoon to a large plate.

Dry the beef cubes with paper towels and sprinkle them with salt and pepper. In batches, sear
the beef in the oil for 3 to 5 minutes, turning to brown on all sides. Remove the meat to the plate
with the bacon and continue searing until all the beef is browned. Set aside.

Toss the carrots, onions, 1 tablespoon of salt and 2 teaspoons of pepper in the fat in the pan
and cook for 10 to 15 minutes, stirring occasionally, until the onions are lightly browned. Add
the garlic and cook for 1 minute. Add the Cognac, stand back, and ignite the liquid with a long
match to burn off the alcohol. Put the meat and bacon back into the pot with the juices. Add the
Cabernet Sauvignon and beef broth; the meat should almost be covered in liquid. Add the tomato
paste and thyme. Bring to a simmer, cover the pot with a tight-fitting lid and cook in the oven for
about 1-¼ hours, or until the meat and vegetables are very tender when pierced with a fork.

Remove the pot from the oven. With a fork, combine 2 tablespoons of butter and the flour and stir
into the stew. Add the frozen onions. In a separate flying pan, sauté the mushrooms in
2 tablespoons of butter for 10 minutes, until lightly browned, then add them to the stew. Bring the
stew to a boil on top of the stove, then lower the heat and simmer for 15 minutes. Season to taste.

To serve, toast the bread slices in the toaster or oven. Rub each slice on 1 side with a cut clove
of garlic. For each serving, spoon the stew over a slice of bread.

pair with fritz cabernet sauvignon

Graton Ridge Cellars

3561 gravenstein highway north, sebastopol, ca 95472
707-823-3040

www.gratonridge.com

There may be no better food match for Pinot Noir than mushrooms; when Pinot Noir is an ingredient in a mushroom dish, the bond becomes even more harmonious. Dust this savory stew with grated Vella Mezzo Secco cheese from Sonoma County. **Serves 6 to 8**

pat's mushroom ragout

with mezzo secco

chef Greg Paulsen, Tasting Room Manager

ingredients

¼ cup olive oil
2 Andouille sausages, diced
8 ounces crimini mushrooms, cleaned and broken into uniform pieces
1 tablespoon unsalted butter
2 to 3 garlic cloves, minced
1 small shallot, minced
½ cup Russian River Valley Pinot Noir
½ cup chicken stock
½ cup heavy cream
salt and pepper
8 ounces Vella Mezzo Secco cheese, shredded
¼ cup chives, snipped

directions

In a large sauté pan, heat the olive oil over medium-low heat. Add the sausages and cook until they're well-browned. Remove the sausages from the pan and set aside. Add the crimini and sauté, stirring frequently, until the mushrooms release their liquid. Increase the heat to medium and continue to cook until the liquid is completely evaporated.

Season the mushrooms with salt and pepper and add the sausage back to the pan, along with the butter, garlic and shallot, and cook for 1 minute. Add the Pinot Noir and simmer until the mixture is thick and syrupy.

Add the chicken stock and continue to simmer, until the liquid is again thick and syrupy. Add the cream, simmer until thick, then taste and correct the seasoning.

Serve the ragout over polenta, topped with the shredded Mezzo Secco and chives.

pair with graton ridge russian river valley pinot noir

Harvest Moon Estate & Winery

2192 olivet road, santa rosa, ca 95401
707-573-8711

www.harvestmoonwinery.com

Here is a sandwich substantial enough to serve for dinner.
Canned chipotle puree can be found in Mexican markets
and most grocery stores. **Serves 4 to 6**

blackened tri-tip sandwich

with caramelized onion and chipotle mayo

chef Jeff Fulwider

ingredients

Tri-Tip
1 3- to 4-pound tri-tip, trimmed of excess fat
1 loaf sourdough French bread, sliced

Chipotle Mayo
1 cup prepared mayonnaise
juice of ½ lime
2 cloves garlic, chopped
pinch of salt
½ bunch cilantro, chopped
2 tablespoons canned chipotle puree

Blackening Spice
½ cup paprika
1 teaspoon dry oregano
½ cup chili powder
1 teaspoon cayenne pepper
1 teaspoon dried thyme
1 teaspoon garlic powder

Caramelized Onions
1 tablespoon olive oil
2 medium onions, cut into matchsticks
pinch of salt

directions

To prepare the chipotle mayonnaise, place all the ingredients in a food processor and blend until smooth. Taste and adjust the seasoning if necessary. Refrigerate until ready to use.

To prepare the tri-tip, first prepare the blackening spice by placing all the ingredients in a small bowl and mixing thoroughly. Liberally salt and pepper the meat, then season more moderately with the spice mixture. Let the tri-tip stand at room temperature for 1 hour, then grill to desired doneness.

To prepare the caramelized onions, in a large frying pan over medium heat, heat the 1 tablespoon of oil. Add the onions and salt, reduce the heat to low and cook for 20 minutes, stirring every 2 minutes, until the onions are golden brown.

To assemble the sandwiches, thinly slice the tri-tip and layer the meat on 1 sourdough bread slice. Spread the chipotle mayo on another slice of bread. Pile caramelized onions on the meat and top with mayo-topped bread slice.

pair with harvest moon russian river valley zinfandel

Hawkes Winery

6734 highway 128, healdsburg, ca 95448
707-433-4295

www.hawkeswine.com

Texas cowboy cooks pride themselves in taking something apparently inedible and transforming it into something delicious. Brisket is the foremost example of this heroic cuisine. Use only a whole brisket and don't get talked into trimming off the fat. Brisket isn't marbled, so it needs an exterior coating of fat to melt down into the lean meat, making it more tender and juicy as it cooks. Serve brisket on paper plates with soft white bread, sliced sour pickles and chopped white onion. On the side, you can offer pinto beans and mustardy potato salad. Anything more is just not right. **Serves 10 to 12**

bc's texas brisket

chef Jake Hawkes

ingredients

Beef Brisket

1 untrimmed beef brisket, about 8 pounds
hickory or mesquite wood chips

Spice Rub

1 tablespoon kosher salt
2 tablespoons sweet paprika
1 tablespoon black pepper
1 teaspoon dried oregano
1 teaspoon dried mustard

directions allow for 7 to 8 hours of cooking time

To prepare the spice rub, in a small bowl, combine all the ingredients.

Preheat a grill to about 250°. Arrange the coals to one side only (brisket does not like direct heat). Add the wood chips.

Clean the brisket and pat it dry. Apply the spice rub to both sides of the meat, rubbing vigorously. Place the brisket, fat side up, in a disposable aluminum roasting pan. Add about 1 cup of water to the pan, or just enough to almost cover the brisket.

Place the pan on the grill, away from the coals. Cover the grill and cook for 7 to 8 hours, adding wood and charcoal as needed. Don't allow the water in the pan to boil; close a vent to lower the heat if necessary. After 4 hours of cooking, turn the brisket over and add more water. The meat is done when a fork easily slides in. Let the meat rest 10 minutes before slicing.

pair with hawkes alexander valley cabernet sauvignon

Holdredge Wines

51 front street, healdsburg, ca 95448
707-431-1424

www.holdredge.com

Ragu is best made earlier in the day or, even better, the day before. This allows the flavors to blossom. Pomegranate molasses is available in Middle Eastern markets and online. I usually make my own by placing pomegranate juice in a saucepan and reducing it to a glaze. It's wonderful drizzled on grilled chicken or lamb, or added to a salad dressing. As an optional serving suggestion, add this duck ragu to pappardelle pasta with a shaving of Pecorino Romano cheese. **Serves 6**

hearty duck ragu

with pinot noir, walnuts and pomegranate

chef Bruce Riezenman, Park Avenue Catering

ingredients

3 whole duck legs
salt and pepper
1 yellow onion, diced
6 large garlic cloves, peeled
1 cup Pinot Noir
2 cups chicken broth
3 bay leaves
2 carrots, peeled and diced

4 celery stalks, peeled and diced
6 sprigs fresh thyme
½ pound potatoes, peeled and diced
1 cup white beans, cooked
2 tablespoons walnut halves, toasted and roughly chopped
1 tablespoon extra virgin olive oil
2 tablespoons pomegranate molasses

directions preheat oven to 350°

Season the duck legs generously with salt and pepper. Place in the refrigerator for at least 30 minutes to an hour. Then pat the legs dry and place them, skin side down, in a heavy-bottomed skillet over medium-low heat. Slowly cook the legs for approximately 10 minutes, until the skin turns golden brown and some of the fat is rendered. Turn the legs and cook for 5 minutes more.

Remove the duck from the pan and pour out all but 1 or 2 tablespoons of fat. Add the onion and garlic, stir, cover and cook for 4 minutes. Add the Pinot Noir and turn the heat to medium-high. Reduce the wine to ¼ the original amount. Add the chicken broth and bay leaves, bring to a simmer and arrange the duck legs in a single layer in the pan. Reduce the heat to low and simmer very slowly for 1 hour, or until the legs are tender yet not falling apart. Gently remove to a glass baking dish.

Skim the excess fat from the top of the broth. Add the carrots, celery, thyme, potatoes and beans. Cover and simmer until the vegetables are fully cooked, about 15 to 20 minutes. Taste and add more salt and pepper if needed. Pour the broth and vegetables over the duck legs.

To serve, carefully remove the legs from the broth and pour/scrape the broth into a sauce pot to reheat. Move the duck to a clean baking dish and place it the preheated oven to let the skin crisp, about 20 to 30 minutes.

Remove the thyme sprigs, spoon the ragu into preheated bowls, and place either a whole piece of duck leg or some of the meat of the leg in the center of each bowl. Drizzle with extra virgin olive oil and pomegranate molasses, then sprinkle generously with toasted walnuts.

pair with holdredge pinot noir

Hop Kiln Winery

6050 westside road, healdsburg, ca 95448
707-433-6491

www.hopkilnwinery.com

Pinot Noir seems to get all the attention when it comes to matching wine with salmon. Yet Chardonnay is Pinot Noir's complementary equal with this pink-fleshed fish, and it's a slam dunk when the salmon is served with sweet local white corn. **Serves 6**

salmone in padella

"salmon in a frying pan"

chef Renzo Veronese

ingredients

6 ears fresh white corn
2 small heads of frisée
4 tablespoons extra virgin olive oil
3 small unpeeled Yukon Gold potatoes, diced
2 large red bell peppers, seeded and diced
¼ cup Hop Kiln HK Generations Chardonnay
6 8-ounce wild salmon fillets

directions preheat oven to 400°

Shuck the corn and cut the kernels off the cobs. Blanch the kernels in boiling water for 5 seconds, then drain. Wash the frisée in cold water and drain thoroughly. Remove the bottom core and cut each head in thirds horizontally.

In a large frying pan, heat 2 tablespoons of olive oil. Add the corn, potatoes and bell peppers. Sauté lightly. Add the wine and let it reduce just a bit. Add the friseé and wilt it for a few seconds only, so that it will stand up on the plate.

In a large ovenproof skillet, heat 2 tablespoons of oil over medium heat and lightly sauté the salmon fillets. Put the pan in the preheated oven for 3 to 4 minutes, or until the fish is cooked to medium-rare. To serve, spoon the vegetable ragout onto plates and top with a salmon fillet.

pair with hop kiln hk generations chardonnay

Inman Family Wines

5793 skylane boulevard, suite c, windsor, ca 95492
707-395-0689

www.inmanfamilywines.com

This recipe was inspired by the flavors I've enjoyed on my visits to the south of France. I created this stew for a Super Bowl party in 2008. It's versatile because it can be kept warm for a long period of time, when you are uncertain of when it will be served. Anchovies are a secret ingredient! I like to serve this stew with a green salad and crusty French bread. It also works well with couscous. **Serves 6 to 8**

provençal chicken stew

chef Kathleen Inman

ingredients

8 to 10 boned chicken thighs, cut into
   bite-sized pieces
1 tablespoon olive oil
4 carrots, diced
4 celery stalks, chopped
3 leeks, sliced (white and pale green parts only)
2 cloves garlic, minced
1 fennel bulb, chopped
   (save the fronds to be added later)
2 pinches saffron
4 anchovy fillets, smashed with a fork

1 bay leaf
3 to 6 sprigs thyme
2 cups chicken stock
2 cups Inman Russian River Valley Pinot Gris
1 red pepper, cut into 2-inch strips
2 tablespoons flat-leaf parsley, chopped
2 tablespoons fennel fronds, chopped
$1/8$ teaspoon cayenne pepper
sea salt to taste
$1/4$ to $1/2$ cup salt-cured black olives
$1/4$ cup parsley minced, for garnish

directions

In a heavy-bottomed pot over medium-high heat, heat the oil and sear the chicken pieces. When they're browned slightly, remove them to a plate and drain the fat from the pot (but don't wipe it out). Reduce the heat to medium, and in the same pot, add the carrots, celery, leeks and garlic and cook for 5 minutes. Add the fennel bulb and chicken and heat through.

Add the saffron, anchovy fillets, bay leaf and thyme sprigs, then stir in the chicken stock and wine. If the liquid doesn't cover the chicken and vegetables, add more stock and/or wine. Place a lid on the pot and simmer for 1 hour.

To the same pot, add the red pepper, parsley, fennel fronds and cayenne pepper. Add sea salt to taste, then simmer for 30 more minutes. Remove the bay leaf and any stems from the thyme. Add the olives and continue to simmer until you're ready to serve the stew. Ladle it into bowls and garnish with minced parsley.

pair with inman rosé of pinot noir "endless crush"

Iron Horse Vineyards

9786 ross station road, sebastopol, ca 95472
707-887-1507

www.ironhorsevineyards.com

Along with world-class Pinot Noir and Chardonnay, Green Valley
is also home to fantastic chestnuts. Around the corner from
Iron Horse Vineyards is the Green Valley Chestnut Ranch, and
its tree-ripened chestnuts are usually available the first two
weeks of October—and pair beautifully with the neighborhood
wines. Here is a simple recipe that celebrates the harvest while
preparing the soul for the holidays. **Serves 4**

braised chicken

with chestnuts

chef Christopher Greenwald, Bay Laurel Culinary

ingredients

4 pounds chicken thighs, cut in half, through the middle of the bone
salt and pepper
3 tablespoons olive oil
1 pound cooked chestnuts, peeled
1-½ ounce piece of fresh ginger, peeled and thickly sliced
2 red onions, peeled and cut into thick matchsticks
4 tablespoons Iron Horse Estate Chardonnay
2 cups roasted chicken stock
1 tablespoon raw sugar
3 to 4 tablespoons soy sauce

directions

Season the chicken with salt and pepper and set aside to marinate. In a large sauté pan (preferably one with sides and a fitting lid), heat the oil on medium-high and add the chestnuts. Sauté for about 5 minutes, or until the chestnuts are golden brown and fragrant. Remove them with a slotted spoon and set aside.

Add the chicken pieces and cook until they're nicely browned. Remove them from the pan. Pour off a little of the fat and add the ginger and onions to the pan. Cook until fragrant, then deglaze the pan with the wine. Reduce the liquid by one-third and add the stock. Bring the liquid to a boil and add the chicken, chestnuts, sugar and soy sauce. Turn the heat down and simmer for about 30 to 45 minutes. If the sauce seems thin, remove the chicken and turn up the heat to reduce the sauce. Check for seasoning and serve over polenta, rice or egg noodles.

pair with iron horse estate chardonnay and pinot noir

Limerick Lane Cellars

1023 limerick lane, healdsburg, ca 95448
707-433-9211

www.limericklanewines.com

Making sausages was one of the most enjoyable things that winery chef Peter Leary learned during his culinary training at Santa Rosa Junior College, and he serves a variety of sausages at Limerick Lane Cellars events. Come to the winery and taste Peter's sausages paired with our wines, and get tips on how to make sausage at home. Ask your local butcher for natural hog casings; they can also be purchased online. **Makes 17 sausages**

housemade
italian sausages
with zinfandel marinara
chef Peter Leary

ingredients

Sausage
3 pounds pork butt
¾ pound pork back or belly fat
¼ cup Limerick Lane Collins Vineyard Zinfandel
1 tablespoon garlic, minced
1 tablespoon red pepper flakes
4 teaspoons kosher salt
2 teaspoons black pepper
1 teaspoon cayenne pepper (optional)
natural hog casings

Zinfandel Marinara
2 28-ounce cans Italian-style tomatoes
2 tablespoons olive oil
5 cloves garlic, chopped
1 medium yellow onion, chopped
1 cup Limerick Lane Collins Vineyard Zinfandel
1 small can tomato paste
1 cup basil leaves, chopped
salt and black pepper to taste

directions

To prepare the sausage, cut the pork butt and pork back/belly fat into 1-inch cubes. Grind in a meat grinder. In a large bowl, add all the other ingredients except for the hog casings and mix by hand. Stuff the sausage into the casings and tie off the casing every 5 inches. Bring a large pot of water to a boil and poach the sausages for 6 minutes. Remove them from the water and grill or pan-fry until they're brown.

To prepare the Zinfandel Marinara, in a large bowl, crush the tomatoes by hand. Heat a large saucepan and add the olive oil. Add the garlic and onion, season with salt and pepper and cook for 3 to 5 minutes. Do not allow the garlic to brown. Add 1 cup of Zinfandel and the tomato paste, and stir to combine. Add the tomatoes and basil. Simmer for at least 2 hours, stirring often and adding water if it becomes too dry. Serve the sausages over pasta or polenta topped with Zinfandel Marinara.

pair with limerick lane zinfandel and syrah

Locals Tasting Room

21023-A geyserville avenue, geyserville, ca 95441
707-857-4900

www.tastelocalwines.com

(Diavola Pizzeria & Salumeria is the new Italian dining spot next door
to Locals in the heart of Geyserville. Opened by executive chef
Dino Bugica of Taverna Santi, also in Geyserville, Diavola practices
the time-honored tradition of "cucina povera," or Italian peasant
specialties. Dino takes pride in his house-cured meats, and his Italian
sweet sausage is featured in this recipe. **Serves 8 to 10**)

hamin brisket of beef

with meatballs

chef Dino Bugica, Executive Chef, Taverna Santi

ingredients

3 pounds Swiss chard
extra virgin olive oil
3-½ cups dried cannellini beans
2 pounds beef brisket
2 Italian sweet sausages, removed from casings and sliced 1 inch thick
2 eggs
1 cup breadcrumbs
1 pound ground chuck
salt and pepper
2 hard-boiled eggs, thin-sliced (for garnish)

directions

Over medium heat, sauté the Swiss chard in a non-stick pan with a little olive oil.

In a Dutch oven, add the cannellini beans with a little water and 1 tablespoon of olive oil, and simmer over low heat for 1 hour. Add the Swiss chard, brisket and sausages. Cover and simmer over very low heat for 4 hours.

Beat the fresh eggs and add them to a large bowl with the bread crumbs, and ground chuck. Mix well and season with salt and pepper. Shape the mixture into balls about the size of walnuts and boil them in a separate pot of water with 1 teaspoon of olive oil. As soon as the meatballs are cooked, add them to the Dutch oven with the beans, chard, brisket and sausages, and coat them in the juices.

To serve, slice the brisket and serve it with the meatballs, sausage and Swiss chard.

pair with your favorite italian-style red wine from locals tasting room

Longboard Vineyards

5 fitch street, healdsburg, ca 95448
707-433-3473

www.longboardvineyards.com

Longboard owner/winemaker Oded Shakked is an ardent surfer, as evidenced by the name he chose for his winery. In a nod to Hawaii, the surfing capital of the world, these kabobs have a Hawaiian sweet-and-spicy flavor, yet are very much at home on the Northern California coast. Find sugar cane skewers or sugar swizzle sticks at gourmet food stores, large liquor stores and online. **Serves 8**

entrées

the bro's killah
beef kabobs

chef Mike Matson, Chef/Owner, Vintage Valley Catering

ingredients

Beef Seasoning
2 ounces Longboard Syrah
2 teaspoons Sriracha chile sauce
2 teaspoons soy sauce
2 tablespoons pineapple juice
½ cup green onions, sliced
2 tablespoons fresh thyme, chopped
2 tablespoons peanut oil

Kabobs
2-½ pounds beef tri-tip, cut into 1-inch cubes
1 whole pineapple, cut into 1-inch cubes
2 Maui onions, cut into 1-inch dice
4 green onions, sliced (for garnish)
8 8-inch sugar cane skewers

directions heat an outdoor or indoor grill

To prepare the beef seasoning, in a small bowl, mix all the ingredients. To prepare the kabobs, coat the beef cubes with the seasoning paste. On each of the 8 sugar cane skewers, thread 5 beef cubes, 5 pineapple cubes and 5 Maui onion pieces, in alternating order. Season the skewers with salt and pepper and grill 5 minutes on each side, or until cooked to desired doneness. Garnish with green onions.

pair with longboard russian river valley syrah

Marimar Estate

11400 graton road, sebastopol, ca 95472
707-823-4365

www.marimarestate.com

(This is a classic Catalan peasant dish from my native Spain, a hearty
main course particularly suitable for buffet dinners—and for hearty
appetites. I don't worry about making too much, because the stew is
even better reheated the next day and freezes wonderfully.
In order to prepare it in Sonoma County, I've made some substitutions
for the traditional Catalan sausages. **Serves 8**)

entrées

catalan-style
lima bean stew
with sausage and fresh mint
chef Marimar Torres

ingredients

2 tablespoons olive oil
½ pound pancetta, julienned
2 medium yellow onions, chopped
4 large garlic cloves, minced
2 10-ounce packages frozen lima beans
1 pound mild pork sausage, such as sweet Italian
1 pound pork blood sausage, such as Italian blood pudding or French boudin noir
3 tablespoons fresh mint, chopped
1 large or 2 small bay leaves
1 cup dry white wine
3 cups chicken stock

directions

In a large, flameproof casserole (preferably made of clay) over low heat, warm the olive oil. Add the pancetta and cook for about 10 minutes. Transfer the pancetta to a small bowl and set aside.

Add the onions and garlic to the casserole and sauté until golden, about 20 minutes. Add the lima beans, toss and cook for 4 or 5 minutes.

Pour about ½ cup of water into a large frying pan and add the sausages. Pierce them with a fork, set the pan over medium-high heat and cook for 3 to 5 minutes, until the water evaporates and sausages are lightly browned. Transfer sausages to a cutting board and cut them into 1-inch slices.

Add the sausages to the casserole along with the pancetta, 1 tablespoon of the chopped mint, the bay leaves and the wine. Add the stock and bring to a boil. Reduce the heat to low and cook, partially covered, for 1 hour or more, until the beans are quite soft.

If the sauce is too thin, uncover the casserole and cook for another 15 minutes, or until the sauce reaches the desired consistency; the stew should be rather soupy. Taste and adjust the seasoning. Just before serving, remove the bay leaves and stir in the remaining 2 tablespoons of mint. Serve in warmed bowls.

pair with marimar estate chardonnay and pinot noir

Martin Ray Winery

2191 laguna road, santa rosa, ca 95401
707-823-2404

www.martinraywinery.com

Our cellarmaster's huge trailer barbecue is a fixture at Martin Ray Winery's harvest parties. This year we share his barbecuing skills with our "A Wine & Food Affair" guests. All weekend long, we'll serve our signature slow-cooked tri-tip marinated in the same Martin Ray Cabernet Sauvignon that we'll pour with our sandwiches. **Serves 6**

wood-smoked

tri-tip sandwiches

with point reyes blue cheese cabernet spread

chef Wendi Hawn

ingredients

Blue Cheese Cabernet Spread

1 cup Point Reyes Blue Cheese
1 stick (4 ounces) unsalted butter, softened
2 tablespoons Martin Ray Cabernet Sauvignon

Tri-Tip and Marinade

3 tablespoons parsley, chopped
2 garlic cloves, peeled
1 teaspoon coarse sea salt
1 cup Martin Ray Cabernet Sauvignon
½ cup extra virgin olive oil
coarsely ground black pepper to taste
1 2- to 3-pound tri-tip beef roast

directions

To prepare the Blue Cheese Cabernet Spread, in a medium bowl, gently mash together all the ingredients with a fork. Refrigerate for several hours or overnight

To prepare the marinade for the tri-tip, add the parsley, garlic and salt to a food processor and blend until the garlic is finely chopped. With the processor running, slowly add the wine, then the olive oil. Place the tri-tip in a glass baking dish and pour the marinade over it. Season the meat with salt and pepper, and let stand at room temperature for at least 30 minutes and up to 1-½ hours.

Heat a grill to medium-high and sprinkle mesquite wood chips on the coals. Remove the tri-tip from the marinade and place the meat on the grill. Sear each side for 5 minutes to seal in the juices, then move the meat to a cooler area on the grill. Cook, turning every 10 minutes or so, until a meat thermometer inserted into the thickest part of the tri-tip registers 130° to 135°. Transfer the meat to a platter and let stand for 10 minutes before thinly slicing the tri-tip against the grain.

To prepare the sandwiches, slice your favorite French loaf lengthwise and toast it on the grill. Immediately spread a thin layer of the blue cheese spread on the warm bread, pile on the tri-tip slices, and serve.

pair with martin ray cabernet sauvignon

Mazzocco Sonoma

1400 lytton springs road, healdsburg, ca 95448
707-431-8159

www.mazzocco.com

What would a Mazzocco event be without skirt steak? Our guests would most likely be greatly disappointed! So skirt steak returns for "A Wine and Food Affair," served with a savory, satisfying butternut squash polenta. **Serves 6 to 8**

barbecued skirt steak

with butternut squash polenta

chef Oui Cater

ingredients

Butternut Squash Polenta

3 butternut squash, cut in half lengthwise and
seeds removed
6 garlic cloves, unpeeled
4 tablespoons olive oil
1 teaspoon dried sage
salt and pepper
2-¾ cups chicken broth
1-¾ cups water
1-½ cups polenta
1 tablespoon fresh sage, minced
¾ cup Parmesan cheese, grated

Marinated Skirt Steak

2 cups soy sauce
¾ cup teriyaki sauce
splash of pineapple juice
splash of Mazzocco Zinfandel
garlic powder to taste
2 strips skirt steak

directions make the polenta 2 to 3 hours in advance

To prepare the polenta, preheat the oven to 375°. Place the squash, cut side up, in a large roasting pan. Put 1 garlic clove in each of the 6 squash halves and brush the surface of the squash with olive oil. Sprinkle with dried sage, salt and pepper. Cover the squash with foil and bake until the flesh is tender, about 1-¼ hours. Remove the squash from the oven and allow to cool slightly.

Peel the squash and garlic, transfer them to a blender or food processor, and puree. Combine the broth, water and 1 teaspoon of salt in a large, heavy-bottomed saucepan. Bring to a boil over high heat. Whisk in the polenta, reduce the heat to medium and cook until the polenta is thick, about 20 minutes. Stir frequently. Add the fresh sage and 3 cups of the squash puree and heat for 2 minutes. Stir in the Parmesan and season with salt and pepper. Place the mixture in a shallow 9x13 baking dish, cover and refrigerate for 2 to 3 hours.

To prepare the skirt steak, in a medium bowl, combine all the ingredients except the meat. Place the two strips of steak in a large glass baking dish and pour the marinade over the meat. Refrigerate for up to 1 hour, but no longer. Preheat a grill on high. Remove the meat from the marinade and grill for 5 minutes, or to desired doneness, turning once midway through the cooking.

To assemble, remove the polenta from the refrigerator and cut it into triangles or squares. Brush each piece with olive oil and grill briefly. Top with slices of skirt steak.

pair with mazzocco zinfandel

The Meeker Vineyard

21035 geyserville avenue, geyserville, ca 95441
707-431-2148

www.meekerwine.com

There is nothing quite like some in-your-face barbecue when you return from traveling the country for winemaker dinners. Inspired by classic barbecue joints like Dinosaur Bar-B-Que in Rochester and Syracuse, NY, and Jack Stack in Kansas City, MO, Molly Meeker created a barbecue sauce that has a sweet and spicy tang and a big Dry Creek Zinfandel kick. After years of experimenting in her kitchen, Molly found the perfect complement to Charlie Meeker's pulled pork.

zinfandel barbecue sauce

chef Molly Meeker

ingredients

¼ cup olive oil
1 cup yellow onion, minced
¼ cup celery, minced
¼ cup carrot, grated
½ cup green bell pepper, minced
1 jalapeno chile, seeded and minced
whole head of garlic, minced
2 14-ounce cans tomato sauce
2 cups ketchup
2 cups Meeker Dry Creek Valley Winemaker's Reserve Zinfandel
¼ cup Worcestershire sauce

½ cup cider vinegar
¼ cup lemon juice
¼ cup molasses
¼ cup spicy brown mustard
¾ cup dark brown sugar, packed
1 tablespoon chili powder
1 tablespoon cayenne pepper
1 teaspoon red pepper flakes
½ teaspoon wasabi powder
2 teaspoons coarse-ground black pepper
½ teaspoon ground allspice

directions

In a large saucepan, add the olive oil and warm over medium heat. Sauté the onion, celery, carrot, green pepper and jalapeno. Season with salt and pepper to taste, and continue to cook until the onions are translucent. Add the garlic and cook for 2 minutes, or until the garlic is soft. Add all the other ingredients, bring the mixture to a boil, then lower the heat to a simmer. Let the sauce thicken to desired consistency and then remove from the heat.

Use the sauce on barbecued meats and vegetarian grilled dishes. We recommend it on ribs or mixed in with Charlie's pulled pork. Charlie uses a classic two-chamber smoker with oak barrel staves, which provides the smoke. He uses a 7- to 8-pound pork butt and smokes it at around 200° for 4 to 5 hours.

pair with meeker winemaker's reserve zinfandel

Mill Creek Vineyards

1401 westside road, healdsburg, ca 95448
707-431-2121

www.millcreekwinery.com

In the dead of winter, we serve this full-flavored, comforting stew over steamed rice or egg noodles. If there is any left over, it's delicious reheated the next day. Montreal Steak Seasoning can be found in most grocery stores. **Serves 6 to 8**

zinfulicious beef zinfandel

chef Yvonne Kreck

ingredients

2 large beef bouillon cubes, or equivalent beef base
1 cup water
1 tablespoon olive oil
2 tablespoons butter
2 pounds round steak, cut into small pieces
1 tablespoon Worcestershire sauce
1 teaspoon Montreal Steak Seasoning
1 medium yellow onion, diced
2 medium leeks, sliced (white and pale green parts only)
4 cloves garlic, minced
1-½ cups Mill Creek Zinfandel
1-½ teaspoons dried Italian seasoning
3 tablespoons flour
2-½ cups fresh mushrooms, sliced
1 can cream of mushroom soup

directions

Dissolve the bouillon cubes in 1 cup of hot water and set aside.

In a very large frying pan, heat the olive oil and butter over medium heat and begin to brown the meat. Sprinkle the pan with Worcestershire sauce and Montreal Steak Seasoning as the beef is browning. When browned, remove the meat to a plate and set aside.

In the same pan, cook the onion, leeks and garlic until they're tender. Return the beef to the pan and stir in the bouillon. Add 1 cup of the Zinfandel. Sprinkle on Italian seasoning and simmer for 1-½ hours, or until the meat is tender. If the mixture gets too dry, add more wine or water to moisten.

In a small bowl, whisk the flour into the remaining ½ cup of wine until smooth, and add it to the pan. Stir in the mushroom soup. Add the mushrooms and cook until they're tender. Serve over rice or noodles.

pair with mill creek vineyards zinfandel

Mounts Family Winery

3901 wine creek road, healdsburg, ca 95448
707-292-8148

www.mountswinery.com

Co-owner Lana Mounts is a first-generation Russian-American. Her paternal and maternal grandparents were born in a small Russian village near the Iranian border. Lana's parents were born and raised in Iran (known then as Persia). Growing up in a large family with many cultural traditions to follow, she was greatly influenced by the diversity of spices and flavors of the Middle East, and incorporates them in her cooking today. Persian and Russian foods were integrated into Lana's life through every celebration, and almost always included marinated lamb and some type of leavened bread. **Serves 4 to 8**

shish lick naane

"marinated lamb kabobs with pita-type bread"

chef Lana Mounts

ingredients

Marinated Lamb
½ cup extra virgin olive oil
½ cup lemon juice
¼ cup honey
4 cloves garlic, minced
½ small yellow onion, minced
¼ cup mint leaves, minced
¼ cup parsley leaves, minced
1 teaspoon rosemary leaves, minced
1 teaspoon oregano leaves, minced
1 teaspoon turmeric powder
1 teaspoon curry powder
1 teaspoon cumin powder
2 pounds boneless lamb leg or shoulder, cut into 1-½-inch cubes
salt and black pepper
16 8-inch skewers (if using wood, soak in water for at least 30 minutes)

Mint Sauce
½ cup mint leaves
¼ cup honey
pinch of kosher salt
2 tablespoons white wine vinegar
freshly ground black pepper
¾ cup extra virgin olive oil

pita bread

directions

To prepare the lamb, in a large bowl, combine all the ingredients except the lamb, salt and pepper, and mix thoroughly. Add the lamb cubes and toss them to coat well. Marinate the lamb in the refrigerator for at least 4 hours, or overnight, if possible.

Preheat a grill or a grill pan on high. Thread the lamb cubes on the skewers. Season the meat with salt and pepper. Grill to desired doneness, about 3 to 5 minutes per side, for medium to medium-rare.

To prepare the mint sauce, in a blender, combine all the ingredients except for the oil, and pulse until well-pureed. With the blender running on low, slowly drizzle in the oil. Taste and adjust the seasonings. Serve the sauce with the kabobs and fresh pita bread.

pair with mounts family syrah, petite sirah and zinfandel

Papapietro Perry Winery

4791 dry creek road, healdsburg, ca 95448
707-433-0422

www.papapietro-perry.com

Chef Bruce Riezenman sometimes puts a whole lamb on a spit, where it cooks for 4 to 6 hours, slowly turning over the fire. Slow-cooking lamb shoulder is the next best thing; it has plenty of fat to keep the meat moist and tender through the slow cooking. Have the butcher remove the bones from the lamb and tie it up as a roast. Most butchers tie with a "net," which can be removed for marinating the meat, then replaced prior to cooking. **Serves 8 to 10**

slow-cooked lamb

with whole corn polenta

chef Bruce Riezenman, Park Avenue Catering

ingredients

Lamb

1 3- to 4-pound lamb shoulder, boneless and tied
1 cup Papapietro Perry Pinot Noir
5 garlic cloves, peeled and sliced
2 sprigs fresh rosemary
¼ cup olive oil
salt and pepper to taste

Polenta

2 ears corn
1 tablespoon butter
¼ yellow onion, minced
3 cups water
1 cup whole milk
1 cup instant polenta
½ cup Parmigiano-Reggiano cheese, grated
1 tablespoon extra virgin olive oil
2 tablespoons butter
kosher salt and white pepper to taste

directions

start one day ahead for both the lamb and polenta

Untie the net on the lamb and open up the meat. Combine remaining ingredients in a mixing bowl. Place the lamb in a baking dish, add the liquid mixture and turn the lamb a few times to coat thoroughly. Cover and marinate the meat in the refrigerator overnight.

To prepare the polenta, shuck the corn, remove all the silk, and cut off all the kernels from both ears. Take the back of the knife and scrape the cobs to release the corn milk onto the pile of kernels. In a medium, heavy-bottomed saucepan, melt 1 tablespoon of butter over medium heat. Add the onion and let it sweat until soft but not brown. Add the corn and corn milk and simmer, covered, for 3 minutes.

Add the milk and water to the pan and bring to a boil. Add a pinch of salt to give the liquid a slight salty taste. Whisk in the polenta. Lower the heat and cook, stirring constantly with a wooden spoon, for 10 to 20 minutes, until the polenta is done (it will still have a slightly gritty texture). Remove the pan from the heat and stir in the cheese, olive oil and remaining 2 tablespoons of butter. Season to taste with the salt and pepper. Pour the polenta into a buttered baking dish so that the layer is ½- to ¾-inch thick. Allow it to cool, then cover with plastic wrap and refrigerate overnight.

Remove the lamb from the marinade and re-tie the meat. If using a rotisserie, skewer the shoulder on the spit and cook it over slow heat for approximately 3 hours, using a pan to catch the drippings. The meat is done when it is golden brown and crisp on the outside, and tender enough to be easily pulled apart.

If using a gas grill, preheat on low; for a charcoal grill, light a small fire of coals on the outer edges of the grill and place the meat in the middle, with no flame directly below. Cover and cook the lamb for the same amount of time as above, until the meat is golden and tender. If cooking the lamb in an oven, preheat to the lowest setting, between 200º and 250º. Place the tied lamb with the marinade in a covered baking dish and roast for 2 hours. Remove the cover, turn the temperature to 300º and cook the meat until very tender. If necessary, add a small amount of water to keep the drippings from drying out (but have no more than a ¼ cup of liquid in the bottom of the pan).

Remove the lamb from the heat, allow it to cool, then pull the meat apart in chunks. Skim the fat from the drippings pan and massage the juices gently into the meat. To serve, preheat the oven to 400º. Cut the polenta into rounds or squares. Remove the cakes to an oiled baking sheet and bake until they are warm and crisp on the outside. Remove them from the oven and top each with a spoonful of the lamb.

pair with papapietro perry pinot noir

Pedroncelli Winery

1220 canyon road, geyserville, ca 95441
707-857-3531

www.pedroncelli.com

When your name is Pedroncelli, you can't help but add Italian-style ingredients to a hearty beef stew. In this winter warmer, we use pancetta (the Italian version of American bacon) and crimini mushrooms (also known as Italian brown mushrooms), and like to serve the stew over soft polenta, or polenta baked into squares. Serves **6**

beef mother clone

chefs Julie Pedroncelli and Ed St. John

ingredients

2 pounds beef stew meat, trimmed and cut into 1-½-inch pieces
flour
salt and black pepper
1 to 1-½ ounces dried porcini mushrooms
1 to 2 tablespoons olive oil
1 large onion, chopped
6 to 8 cloves garlic
1 ounce salted pancetta, diced
1 pound crimini mushrooms, sliced
2 cups beef broth
2 cups Pedroncelli Mother Clone Zinfandel

directions preheat oven to 350°

Roll the beef cubes in flour that has been seasoned with salt and black pepper, and set aside. Soak the dried mushrooms in enough hot water to cover for 20 minutes, strain, and save the soaking water and mushrooms.

Heat a Dutch oven on medium-high heat. Pour 1 tablespoon of olive oil into the pan, add the onion, and sauté for 5 minutes. Add the garlic and sauté until golden brown. Remove the onion/garlic mixture and set aside.

Cook the pancetta in the Dutch oven until the pancetta is crisp. Remove the pancetta and set it aside. Add the floured beef cubes and brown on all sides; do this in batches, without crowding the pan, in order to achieve even browning. Remove the browned beef and set aside.

In the same pan, add the sliced crimini mushrooms and sauté for 3 minutes. Add the onion mixture, pancetta, meat, beef broth, Zinfandel, and the hydrated porcini mushrooms and their liquid, to the pan. Cover tightly and cook in the oven for 1 to 1-½ hours, then serve.

pair with pedroncelli mother clone zinfandel

Selby Winery

215 center street, healdsburg, ca 95448
707-431-1288

www.selbywinery.com

The sweet and tangy taste of our barbecue sauce perfectly complements the bold berry flavors of Selby Old Vines Zinfandel. While this sauce is delicious with our mini meatball subs, it's also great with chicken wings, burgers and pulled pork. Once prepared, the sauce will keep in the refrigerator for several weeks. **Serves 4**

entrées

mini-meatball subs

with selby old vines zinfandel barbecue sauce

ingredients

Zinfandel Barbecue Sauce

2 tablespoons olive oil
2 cloves garlic, minced
¼ cup green onions, minced
½ cup yellow onion, minced
2 cups Selby Old Vines Zinfandel
2 cups ketchup
3/4 cup dark brown sugar
4 tablespoons honey
4 tablespoons Worcestershire sauce
½ tablespoon orange juice concentrate
2 tablespoons Dijon mustard
1 tablespoon prepared yellow mustard
1 teaspoon chili powder
dash or two bottled hot sauce

Selby Meatballs

2 pounds ground beef
1 cup fresh bread crumbs
½ cup grated Parmesan cheese
1 heaping tablespoon fresh basil, chopped
1 heaping tablespoon fresh parsley, chopped
1 teaspoon kosher salt
½ teaspoon black pepper
$1/8$ teaspoon cayenne pepper
2 cloves garlic, minced
2 eggs
3 tablespoons olive oil

4 soft sandwich rolls, toasted

directions

To prepare the barbecue sauce, in a large saucepan pan, heat the olive oil over medium heat until it's hot but not smoking. Add the garlic and sauté for 10 seconds. Add green and yellow onions and sauté for an additional 30 seconds. Add the Zinfandel and raise the heat. Bring to a boil. Once boiling, reduce the heat and simmer the sauce until the wine reduces by half.

Add all the remaining ingredients to the pan and slowly bring to a boil. Reduce the heat and simmer for 15 minutes, or until the sauce has thickened to a desired consistency. Refrigerate until ready to use.

To prepare the meatballs, in a large bowl, add all the ingredients except the olive oil, using your hands to gently blend the components. Roll the meat between your palms into balls about 2 inches in diameter, firmly packing but not compressing the meat (yields about 16 meatballs).

In a large, heavy pot, heat the oil over medium-high heat. When it shimmers, add the meatballs in batches, taking care not to overcrowd the pan. Brown well on the bottoms of each meatball before turning, or they will break apart. Continue cooking until browned all over. Remove the meatballs to a plate and let them cool slightly. Cover and refrigerate until needed.

To assemble the mini-meatball subs, reheat the meatballs, place them on 4 toasted submarine rolls and slather on the Old Vines Zinfandel Barbecue Sauce.

pair with selby old vines zinfandel

Sheldon Wines

6761 sebastopol avenue, #500, sebastopol, ca 95472
707-829-8100

www.sheldonwines.com

The pizza dough is quick and easy to make, as you don't have to wait for it to rise. The original recipe dates to the 14th century in the Emilia-Romagna region of Italy. It started out as a pasta recipe, and we began using it for thin, delicate ravioli. One night Tobe suggested we try to make a Northern Italian-style, thin-crust pizza with the recipe ... and the wine pizza was born! You can substitute Chardonnay for the Petite Sirah in the dough recipe and omit the tomato sauce, giving you a "white" pizza to be topped by ingredients of your choice. **Makes 2 pizzas**

entrées

petite sirah pizzahh

chef Dylan Sheldon

ingredients

Super Simple Pizza Sauce

10 medium tomatoes, tops cut off and
    seeds removed with a spoon
10 cloves garlic
1 tablespoon balsamic vinegar
2 to 3 tablespoons extra virgin olive oil
1 tablespoon oregano, coarsely chopped
10 basil leaves, cut into ribbons
sea salt, to taste
black pepper, to taste
red pepper flakes, to taste

Pizza

1-¼ cups unbleached, all-purpose flour
½ cup Sheldon Petite Sirah wine
big pinch sea salt
Super Simple Pizza Sauce
½ cup Parmigiano-Reggiano cheese, grated
prosciutto, thinly sliced
½ cup pine nuts

directions preheat oven to 350°

First prepare the Super Simple Pizza Sauce. Place a garlic clove in each scooped-out tomato. Roast the tomatoes for 30 minutes. Transfer the tomatoes, their juice and garlic to a saucepan and mash the mixture with a wooden spoon. Over low heat, stir in the balsamic vinegar, oil and oregano, and cook for 8 minutes. Add the basil and reduce the mixture for 2 to 3 minutes. Add the salt, black pepper and pepper flakes to taste. Cover and let stand.

To prepare the dough, increase the oven temperature to 375°. In a bowl, blend the flour, wine and salt and knead by hand for 10 minutes. The dough should become satiny and very elastic. Use only enough flour so that the dough is as soft as possible, yet no longer sticking to your fingers. Divide the dough in half and roll 1 out as thin as possible on a well-floured surface. Place the dough on a non-stick, perforated pizza pan (or two pans for two pizzas).

Spread just enough sauce on the dough to cover (be sure to get the edges). Generously grate Parmigiano-Reggiano over the pizza. Top with prosciutto slices and a scattering of pine nuts, and bake on the second rack from the top of the oven. It should take 9 to 12 minutes for the crust to turn dark golden brown and blister a bit. Slice and serve.

pair with your favorite sheldon wine

Suncé

on the Healdsburg Plaza
132 plaza street, healdsburg, ca 95448 707-433-2021

Winery & Vineyard
1839 olivet road, santa rosa, ca 95401 707-526-9463

www.suncewinery.com

Get out the crockpot for this recipe, which is an easy,
fool-proof way to slow-cook beef. Slather the zesty barbecue
sauce on sourdough rolls, add the beef and you've got
a delicious, red-wine-friendly sandwich **Serves 6 to 8**

suncé barbecued

beef sandwiches

chef Denise Stewart

ingredients

Beef

½ teaspoon garlic salt
½ teaspoon seasoned salt
½ teaspoon black pepper
½ teaspoon onion powder
½ teaspoon paprika
½ teaspoon dark chili powder
2 tablespoons dry mustard
5 pounds beef chuck roast
1 12-ounce bottle beer
soft sourdough French rolls

Barbecue Sauce

1 32-ounce bottle Heinz ketchup
2 cups water
½ cup golden brown sugar
¼ cup Worcestershire sauce
2 tablespoons lemon juice
½ teaspoon Tabasco sauce

directions

To prepare the beef, in a small bowl, mix all of the dry seasonings together. Rub the mixture all over the chuck roast. Pour the beer into a large crockpot and add the seasoned beef. Cook on high overnight.

The next day, turn off the crockpot, remove the meat to a large bowl and shred it with your fingers, removing any fat and gristle. Prepare the barbecue sauce, mixing all the ingredients together in a large saucepan and simmering over low heat for 35 minutes.

To assemble the sandwiches, pour the barbecue sauce over the shredded beef and mix well. Reheat the meat and spoon it into soft sourdough French rolls.

pair with suncé barbera

desserts & sweets

Balletto Vineyards & Winery

5700 occidental road, santa rosa, ca 95401
707-568-2455

www.ballettovineyards.com

This recipe comes from a great family friend, Mia Del Prete. Her great grandmother, Nonna Del Rosso, was born near Lucca, Italy. She and her two sisters came to America in 1908 to join their parents, who had settled in a small town known as Largo, between Hopland and Ukiah, in Mendocino County. Mia remembers going as a small child to visit Nonna Del Rosso, who always had a fresh batch of biscotti waiting and a small glass of red wine in which she could dip her cookie. When Mia was old enough to cook, her nonna showed her how to make this recipe. **25 to 30 biscotti**

nonna del rosso's
biscotti

chef Mia Del Prete

ingredients

²/₃ cup butter, creamed
3 eggs, beaten
1 teaspoon vanilla
3 teaspoons fresh lemon juice
1-½ cups granulated sugar
3 cups all-purpose flour
2-½ teaspoons baking powder
1 teaspoon anise seed
1 cup almonds, chopped
cooking spray

directions preheat oven to 350°

Mix butter, eggs, vanilla and lemon juice in a large bowl for 1 minute. In a separate bowl, combine all the dry ingredients and blend with a fork. Add the dry ingredients to the butter mixture and mix well.

Spray a cookie sheet lightly with cooking spray. Shape the mixture into 5 to 8 small oblong loaves and place onto the cookie sheet, leaving 1 inch between loaves. Bake for approximately 25 to 30 minutes, or until the loaves are just brown around the edges. Remove the loaves from the oven and allow to cool.

Slice loaves into half-moon-shaped cookies, approximate 1 inch wide. If you prefer harder biscotti, brown them under the broiler until they're toasted on each side.

pair with balletto late harvest pinot gris and balletto zinfandel

Camellia Cellars

57 front street, healdsburg, ca 95448
707-433-1290

www.camelliacellars.com

Bruce and I were in Colorado to pour wine at the Taste of Vail
event when I came upon this recipe from the Junior League
of Denver. I tried it out at a friend's kitchen there, and served
it to some of the local restaurateurs with our Cabernet
Sauvignon. It was a great hit! The cake is very moist and
freezes well. The fondue can be refrigerated, then reheated
for use. I also brought back a Golden Retriever puppy, Mario.
While he can't have the cake, he sure enjoys the aromas
from the kitchen when I bake it. **Serves 12 to 16**

desserts & sweets

chocolate pound cake

with white chocolate-hazelnut fondue

chef Chris Lewand

ingredients

Chocolate Pound Cake

1-½ cups unsalted butter, softened
3 cups granulated sugar
2 teaspoons vanilla extract
5 large eggs
1 cup unsweetened cocoa powder
2 cups all-purpose flour
½ teaspoon baking powder
½ teaspoon salt
1 cup buttermilk
¼ cup water

White Chocolate-Hazelnut Fondue

15 ounces white chocolate, chopped
¾ cup heavy cream
1 tablespoon hazelnut liqueur
1 teaspoon vanilla extract
½ cup hazelnuts, toasted and chopped

directions preheat oven to 325°

To prepare the cake, in a large mixing bowl, cream together the butter and sugar. Beat at high speed for 5 minutes, then add the vanilla. Add the eggs, one at a time, beating well after each addition.

In a separate bowl, mix together the cocoa powder, flour, baking powder and salt. To the butter mixture, add the dry mixture alternately with the buttermilk and water, ending with the dry ingredients. Mix until blended well. Pour into a greased and floured 10-inch tube pan and bake for 60 to 75 minutes, or until a wooden toothpick inserted into the center comes out clean. Let the cake rest in the pan for 20 minutes, then turn out onto a cake rack. Allow to cool thoroughly.

To prepare the fondue, place the white chocolate in a large bowl and put it in a pan of hot water to slowly melt the chocolate. In a small saucepan, bring the heavy cream to a boil; pour over the white chocolate, stirring until smooth. Stir in the liqueur, vanilla and hazelnuts. This can be covered and refrigerated. To reheat, warm in the microwave until the fondue is just soft enough to spoon onto the cake.

Slice the cake and drizzle fondue over each piece.

pair with camellia cellars cabernet sauvignon

Chateau Felice Winery

10603 chalk hill road, healdsburg, ca 95448
707-431-9010

www.chateaufelice.com

This recipe comes from Cena Luna restaurant chefs Yvette Peline-Hom and Stuart Hom, partners in life and in the kitchen. One of Chateau Felice vintner Samantha Rodgers' favorite wines for an after-work meal and dessert is our Acler Chardonnay. Be sure to have three round, 9-inch springform pans ready before starting this recipe. **Serves 8**

cena luna
lemon cake

chefs Yvette Peline-Hom and Stuart Hom, Cena Luna

ingredients

Lemon Curd

15 egg yolks
5 whole eggs
2-½ cups sugar
1-½ cups fresh Meyer lemon juice
pinch of salt
4 tablespoons unsalted butter

Lemon Cake

1 cup unsalted butter, softened
2 cups granulated sugar
4 large eggs
1-½ cups self-rising flour
1-¼ cups all-purpose flour
¾ cup milk
¼ cup fresh Meyer lemon juice
1 teaspoon lemon zest

Whipped Cream

3 cups heavy cream
¼ cup sugar
1 teaspoon vanilla extract

directions make the lemon curd 1 day in advance

For the curd, in a stainless steel bowl, whisk together all the ingredients except the butter and place the bowl atop a pot of boiling water. Cook, stirring occasionally, until the curd is thick enough that it makes "trails" when the whisk is pulled through it. Remove the bowl from the heat, whisk in the butter and stir until it's melted. Put the mixture into a clean container, cover with plastic wrap and refrigerate overnight.

For the cake, preheat the oven to 350°. Cream the butter until smooth. Add the sugar gradually and beat until fluffy, about 3 minutes. Add the eggs one at a time, stirring after each addition. Combine the 2 flours and add them to the mixture in 3 additions, alternating with the milk, lemon juice and lemon zest. Beat well after each addition. Divide the batter evenly into the 3 springform pans and bake for 20 to 25 minutes. Let cool for 10 minutes, then remove to a cake rack.

To assemble, remove the curd from the refrigerator. Cut off the top of the 3 cakes so that each cake is of equal thickness. Divide the curd in half. In a bowl, whip the heavy cream, sugar and vanilla to stiff peaks. Fold in half of the lemon curd.

Spread a thin layer of the remaining lemon curd on the top of each cake, followed by a layer of the whipped lemon cream. Stack the 3 cakes on top of each other, then ice the top with the remaining lemon cream.

Refrigerate at least 3 hours before serving.

pair with chateau felice acier chardonnay

Truett Hurst Winery

5610 dry creek road, healdsburg, ca 95448
707-433-9545

www.truetthurst.com

We took this decadent recipe from our friends
at the Downtown Bakery & Creamery in
Healdsburg and adapted it for use with our
vintage port. **48, 2-inch-square pieces**

dark chocolate brownies

studded with port-soaked cherries

ingredients

½ cup dried cherries, chopped
½ cup Truett Hurst Port
3 sticks unsalted butter
12 ounces unsweetened chocolate, chopped
3 cups granulated sugar
6 large eggs, lightly beaten
1 teaspoon vanilla extract
1 teaspoon almond extract
2-¼ cups all-purpose flour, sifted
½ teaspoon salt

directions preheat oven to 325°

In a small saucepan, combine the chopped cherries and port. Bring to a boil and cook for 30 seconds. Take the pan off the heat and allow the mixture to cool to room temperature, then strain. Discard the liquid.

Spray a 12x17 inch, half-sheet pan with nonstick spray. Line the bottom of the pan with parchment paper and spray the paper.

In a large saucepan, melt the butter and chocolate over low heat, stirring often. Remove the pan from the heat and stir in the sugar. Add the eggs quickly and stir to avoid "scrambling" them. Add the vanilla and almond extracts and stir to combine.

Mix in the flour and salt. Add the strained cherries and stir to combine. Pour the brownie mixture onto the prepared sheet pan, level the height and smooth the top. Bake on the center rack of the oven for 25 minutes. Allow to cool in the sheet pan before cutting into 2-inch squares.

pair with truett hurst port

recipe index

by winery and lodging
the wineries

recipe index

by winery and lodging

the wineries continued

recipe index

by winery and lodging
the wineries continued

recipe index

by winery and lodging
the lodgings

our sponsors

Calistoga brand water is a proud sponsor of all three Russian River Wine Road events!

Calistoga® Brand Mountain Spring Water, sourced from the Mayacamas, Sierra Nevada and Palomar mountains, has a refreshing, crisp, clean taste, and is available in a variety of convenient bottle sizes.

Calistoga Sparkling Juices are a refreshing blend of certified organic fruit juices, organic natural cane sugar, other natural ingredients and our famous mineral water. Perfectly balanced, not-too-sweet premium sparkling juices are precisely what our consumers have been clamoring for: all-natural Calistoga Sparkling Juices in a new premium bottle and with a refreshing new look.

Going Green(er) At events, the Russian River Wine Road will reduce plastic waste by providing Calistoga drinking water from refillable, pump-able multi-gallon containers. Guests can dispense the water directly into their event wineglasses.

KGO Radio has been the most listened-to radio station in Northern California for nearly 30 years, providing intensive live and local coverage. Its award-winning news team delivers local, national and international news seven hours a day and a dynamic and distinguished group of talk show hosts keep the region informed, entertained and connected. KGO Radio has a forceful commitment to the community, raising millions of dollars for the Leukemia and Lymphoma Society for Cancer Research, and supporting organizations that provide food and shelter for the homeless and hungry.

KGO Radio personality Gene Burns fully reflects the station's format and passion. During the week he is a fiery, issue-driven News Talk host with the No. 1 talk program in his time slot. On Saturdays, he hosts a top-rated wine and food show, **Dining Around With Gene Burns**, and is considered the Bay Area's leading gourmand, regularly called upon to assist in fund-raising efforts. Mr. Burns can be heard weekdays from 7 p.m. to 10 p.m., and Saturdays from 10 a.m. to 1 p.m.
www.kgoam810.com

another great food & wine pairing

Russian River Wine Road Donates $30k To Local Food Bank
Making it the Largest Winery Association Donor

Healdsburg, CA (May 8, 2008)—On Thursday, May 1, 2008, the Russian River Wine Road's executive director, Beth Costa, and president, Nancy Woods, presented the Redwood Empire Food Bank with a portion of the proceeds from this year's 30th annual Barrel Tasting. Over 100 wineries located in Dry Creek, Russian River, and Alexander Valleys threw open their cellar doors to celebrate this year's Barrel Tasting and over the two weekend event raised an impressive $30,000 for the Food Bank.

Nancy Woods, David Goodman and Beth Costa.

The Food Bank serves 50,000 people in Sonoma, Mendocino, Lake, Humboldt, and Del Norte Counties each month, including children, seniors, and working families. "The Wine Road is proud to support the Food Bank and in turn those in need in the community. We are so proud of the fact that our contributions to this organization over the last 18 months now totals $70,000, making us the largest winery association donor," says Beth Costa, "Something our members can truly be proud of."

The Russian River Wine Road is an association of 150 wineries and 50 lodgings throughout the Alexander, Dry Creek, Russian River, Chalk Hill, and Green Valley regions in Northwest Sonoma County, a stunning landscape dotted with wineries and picturesque towns. The grandeur of the Pacific Ocean and towering redwoods lead you inland along quiet country roads only one hour north of San Francisco. And…there is always something going on along the "Wine Road" with year-round winery events, exciting new releases of wine and much more. For more information or to request a free map, contact Beth Costa at 800.723.6336 or email info@wineroad.com. Please visit the website at www.wineroad.com.

In addition to the donation from Barrel Tasting, $1.00 for every ticket sold for A Wine & Food Affair, as well as a portion of the poster sales from Barrel Tasting, are donated to the Redwood Empire Food Bank. For more information about REFB or to make a donation, please log onto www.refb.com.

REDWOOD EMPIRE
FOOD BANK

what is the wine road?

Wending through some of the most picturesque country in California, the Russian River Wine Road takes visitors on a sensually gratifying journey of natural beauty, sublime tasting experiences and memorable personal encounters with the state's most devoted and individualistic winemakers. Even for veteran travelers well-acquainted with California wine country, the Wine Road is likely to be uncharted territory, sure to provide a fresh sense of discovery. Along the route are some of California's oldest wineries, operated by vintners whose commitment to tending their vines and producing world-class wines goes back generations.

Founded more than 30 years ago, the Russian River Wine Road is an association of wineries and lodgings in the Alexander, Dry Creek and Russian River Valleys in Northwest Sonoma County. From its modest beginning as a group of nine wineries, the organization has grown into a spirited constellation of more than 140 wineries and 50 lodgings. It's not actually a "road" in the sense of a single, continuous stretch of paved highway, but rather a treasure map to the many jewels nestled in the hills and valleys of a region where fresh air, fine wine and exquisite cuisine await those who traverse it.

This lively and committed association has created myriad programs, events and services certain to enhance any visitor's stay in the region, among them three major events: Winter Wineland, Barrel Tasting, and A Wine & Food Affair (schedules and more information can be found at www.wineroad. com). A complimentary Wine Road map is the key to exploring the glories of the area and is also available online at www.wineroad.com.

regional information

Immigrants make their mark

The region is nothing if not rich in history. The Russian River takes its name from the Russian fur trappers who established a trading colony in the early 19th century; following on their heels were French and Italian immigrants who brought their centuries-old traditions of winemaking to the area. Wine has been made in Sonoma County for more than 130 years. Even during the Prohibition years (1920-1933), many wineries continued to make wine for medicinal and sacramental purposes.

The Russian River itself meanders through three AVAs whose vineyards represent a pastiche of micro-climates and soils that yield a startling diversity of ultra-premium wine varietals. Each appellation has its stars: Russian River Valley's are Pinot Noir and Chardonnay; Dry Creek Valley is known for Zinfandel and Sauvignon Blanc; and Alexander Valley is home to fine Merlot and Cabernet Sauvignon. Yet dozens of other grape varieties are grown in all these regions, including Barbera, Carignane, Dolcetto, Gewurztraminer, Grenache, Riesling, Sangiovese, Syrah and Viognier, to name just a few.

The region's winemaking traditions were forged in large part by Italian immigrants who planted a mix of their favorite grape varieties, which to this day are made into interesting field blends not to be found elsewhere. This early Italian influence is still very much in evidence at venerable establishments such as Simi Winery, founded by Giusseppe and Pietro Simi in Healdsburg in 1876, and Seghesio Family Vineyards, started by Edoardo and Angela Seghesio in 1895 with the planting of their first vineyards.

Tradition meets modernity

Yet the Russian River Wine Road is also where modern, state-of-the-art wineries such as Kendall-Jackson and Ferrari-Carano co-exist with small, artisanal producers for whom making wine is a way of life, intertwined with the responsibilities of home and family. From Italian-style villas to French-style chateaux to small garagistes (a term coined because many began making wine in their garages), the Russian River Wine Road provides a kaleidoscopic view into the world of winemaking. This makes traveling the Wine Road not only a wine experience, but a personal experience.

There are plentiful picnic areas, with many wineries offering patios, decks and gardens for leisurely lunches, and wine-worthy food available for takeaway at such beloved eateries as the Dry Creek General Store and the Jimtown Store. A trip along the Russian River Wine Road breathes new life into the poet Omar Khayyam's notion of the ingredients for a perfect moment: "A jug of wine, a loaf of bread, and thou."

events

Russian River Wine Road Annual Events

Winter Wineland
January – Every Martin Luther King Jr. birthday weekend

Meet the winemakers, taste new releases and library wines, enjoy food pairings and tour wineries during this annual cold-weather warmer. Purchase tickets and get detailed information about the program on our web site, approximately two months prior to the event. Typically, 100 wineries participate in Winter Wineland.

Barrel Tasting
March – The first two weekends

This is your opportunity to go into the cellar to sample wines directly from the barrel and purchase "futures"—wines that are still in barrel or bottle and not yet available in the marketplace. Many wineries sell futures at a discount, and invite buyers to return when the wine is bottled (typically 12 to 18 months later) to pick up their purchases. Many wines are so limited that buying futures is the only way to obtain them. Tickets will be available online approximately two months prior to the event, which usually includes 100 wineries.

A Wine & Food Affair
November – The first full weekend

This is Russian River Wine Road's premiere event—a full weekend of wine and food pairings, with each attendee receiving the current volume of our cookbook and an event logo glass. Each of the approximately 75 participating wineries provides a favorite recipe for the cookbook, and prepares that dish both days for you to sample with the perfect wine. Many Wine Road lodgings also showcase recipes for their best dishes. Ticket and program information will be available online two months in advance of the event.

(For details on these annual events and other wine country festivities sponsored by our members, visit

www.wineroad.com)

american viticultural areas (AVAs)
we represent

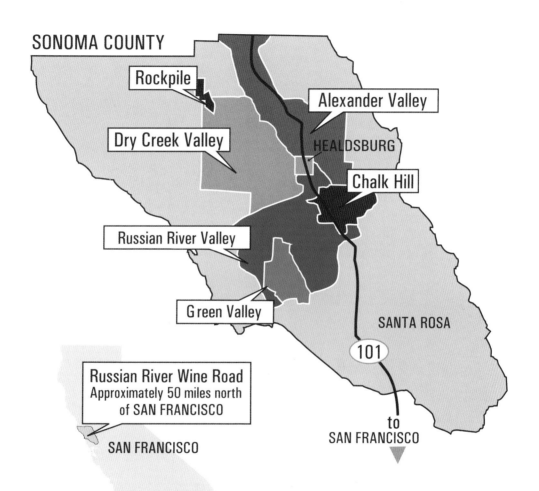

SONOMA COUNTY

Rockpile

Dry Creek Valley

Alexander Valley

HEALDSBURG

Chalk Hill

Russian River Valley

Green Valley

SANTA ROSA

101

Russian River Wine Road
Approximately 50 miles north
of SAN FRANCISCO

SAN FRANCISCO

to
SAN FRANCISCO

Russian River Wine Road
Northwest Sonoma County